LINKING LITERATURE & COMPREHENSION

Integrating Literature Into Basic Skills Programs

by Shirley Cook

Incentive Publications, Inc.
Nashville, Tennessee

Illustrated by Marta Johnson
Cover by Tony Novak
Edited by Jan Keeling

ISBN 0-86530-205-7

TABLE OF CONTENTS

February

Animals and More Animals

SPRING
March

Fables, Tales, and Legends

PREFACE

LINKING LITERATURE AND COMPREHENSION contains integrated literature and writing activities designed for use in the primary classroom in conjunction with selected children's books. The major focus of the systematic model of instruction presented throughout this book is to promote the enjoyment of reading; to develop increased vocabularies; to enhance writing skills; to expand thinking skills; and to encourage a healthy self-concept. Because the activities offer practical applications of integrated curriculum in the areas of reading, writing, and thinking, the teacher will find it easy to implement literature activities for all students!

Emphasizing literature in the primary grades is highly valuable. Literature enables students to enjoy stories with lasting value, to experience rich vocabulary, and to learn to share ideas with others. By responding to what they read, write, and think, students develop and hone critical and creative thinking skills. Literature also serves as a written model for young writers by concretely illustrating how to put thoughts on paper. Primary students need to experience the sense of authorship. As students write, they practice the skill of effectively communicating with an audience as well as gain an appreciation of the value of learning process skills. After continued reading of quality literature, individuals often begin to experiment and practice new writing techniques. What's more, creative illustrations which frequently accompany juvenile literature can captivate students' imaginations, and motivate them to explore their own capabilities.

Effective language arts instruction is dependent upon the teacher's ability to "connect" literature and writing. LINKING LITERATURE AND COMPREHENSION contains the resources necessary to help students develop a holistic approach to reading and writing. These highly motivational activities will promote positive attitudes and improve the self-concept of every student!

HOW TO USE THIS BOOK

LINKING LITERATURE AND COMPREHENSION is designed to help children think critically about the stories they are reading. Bloom's Taxonomy of higher level thinking has been integrated into the questions and activities for each story.

To gain maximum effectiveness from the materials in this book, teachers will need to work on the following skills with their students.

1. **Brainstorming techniques** (generating countless ideas on one topic): During the initial brainstorming, no ideas are thrown out or considered unimportant. Lists may be narrowed at a later time.
2. **Writing a paragraph:** Children should be aware of a main idea and the importance of paragraphing.
3. **Research techniques:** Children must know where reference books are located and be somewhat familiar with them.

In order to gauge the appropriateness of a piece of literature for a child's reading level, it is helpful to scan the listed vocabulary words.

TEACHER PAGES

Every teacher page is labeled with the month and theme, and contains the following components.

Summary
To quickly familiarize yourself with the selected book, read the brief story summary.

Vocabulary
Review the vocabulary words with the class before reading the story. Students may write the words in vocabulary word books and "define" the words with pictures, sentence games, synonyms, etc.

Setting Reading Purpose
To pique interest and encourage attention to the story, discuss these questions with the class before reading.

Questions During Reading
These may be discussed at key moments during the reading of the story or after the story is completed.

Comprehension Skill Extenders
These activities involving research, writing, discussion, and illustration will further develop comprehension skills.

Curriculum Integration
As the need for a creative project arises, implement the suggested curriculum integration activity inspired by the story.

STUDENT PAGES

Some of the teacher pages are followed by reproducible student pages to be used in conjunction with the story. These pages are intended for reproduction and can be identified by this statement:

One highly successful way the contents of this book may be used is to prepare the sections to be placed at a learning center. They may then be used during seatwork, free time, or as enrichment alternatives to workbook pages within the basal reading program. For each book, you will need a pocket folder. On the front of the pocket folder laminate the Vocabulary and Setting Reading Purpose components; inside the folder laminate the Questions During Reading section (black out the answers to the questions before laminating); then laminate the Comprehension Skill Extenders and Curriculum Integration activities onto separate cards and place them inside the pocket folder along with the book itself. Include STUDENT PAGES when applicable. You may choose to record *half* the story on tape to be placed in the folder along with the activity cards and the book.

Children may also read the books as a cooperative group and complete the activity cards and the book.

It is important to make nonchapter books available at all times to enable less-able readers to feel less self-conscious about their abilities. At the same time, many nonchapter books offer a rich wealth of vocabulary and limitless opportunity for thinking skills development.

SEPTEMBER

Dinosaurs and Dragons

DINOSAURS ARE DIFFERENT
by Aliki

Summary

Factual explanations of the differences and similarities of various suborders of dinosaurs.

Vocabulary

1. skeletons	5. pelvic	9. ornithopods
2. hips	6. dentary	10. dome
3. saurischian	7. predentary	11. ceratopsians
4. ornithischian	8. theropods	12. hadrosaurs

Setting Reading Purpose

1. Dinosaurs were alike and different in many ways. There were not any cameras around when they roamed the earth. How do scientists know so much about dinosaurs?
2. Name one dinosaur that did not eat meat. How do you know it was not a meat eater?

Questions During Reading

1. (literal) What is a Saurischian? (It is a lizard-hipped dinosaur.)
2. (inferential) How could you tell the difference between a Saurischian and an Ornithischian by looking at its skeleton? (The Saurischian has one pelvic bone pointing forward and one pointing backward. The Ornithischian has two pelvic bones pointing backward.)
3. (literal) What kind of a jawbone do reptiles have? (Dentary.)
4. (inferential) To what suborder did Diplodocus belong? (Sauropoda.)

Comprehension Skill Extenders

1. Create a list of all the Sauropods you can find. Use as many reference books as you need.
2. If you had to be a dinosaur for a month and travel in a time machine back to the time of dinosaurs, what kind of a dinosaur would you choose to be? Support your choice.
3. Design a new line of sneakers that features dinosaur pictures. Draw the three best-selling tennis shoes in your collection on an ad designed to sell your product. Be sure to include the price and tell where the shoes can be purchased.

Curriculum Integration

Write a poem about your favorite dinosaur. Then write a poem about your least-favorite dinosaur. Do not give the names of the dinosaurs in either poem. Read your poems to a friend in the class to see if he/she can guess the names of the dinosaurs you wrote about.

DIGGING UP DINOSAURS
by Aliki

Summary

A factual tale of methods used by scientists who preserve and study dinosaur bones written in simplified terms.

Vocabulary

1. museum	7. fierce	12. preserved	18. grit
2. apatosaurus	8. Tyrannosaurus	13. patiently	19. shellac
3. corythosaurus	Rex	14. experts	20. draftsman
4. iguanodon	9. continent	15. quarries	21. fiberglass
5. triceratops	10. extinct	16. canyons	22. original
6. stegosaurus	11. fossil	17. site	

Setting Reading Purpose

1. Museums in many parts of the country have dinosaur skeletons on display. How did those skeletons get into the museums? After a dinosaur bone is discovered, what happens to it?
2. Not all dinosaur skeletons on display are real. What are some dinosaur skeletons made from?

Questions During Reading

1. (literal) To prove that she's not afraid of the dinosaurs in the museum, what does the little girl say under her breath? ("...you bag of bones...")
2. (inferential) How many continents are there on earth? (Seven.)
3. (literal) How long has it been since dinosaurs have been around? (65 million years.)
4. (inferential) From what type of dinosaur did the very first fossils come? (Iguanodon.)

Comprehension Skill Extenders

1. Do some research to find out which museums in the country have the largest displays of dinosaurs. If you could go to any museum that you wanted to and study dinosaurs for a week, which museum would you choose? Why?
2. Pretend that you are a paleontologist who has just arrived at the scene of an enormous new dinosaur discovery. Write your diary entries for one week. Include the highlights of each day.
3. Dinosaur bones are carefully dug out of the ground. List other items that are also dug out of the ground.

Curriculum Integration

Turn time back 65 million years. Choose a favorite dinosaur. Create a baby book to outline the events of your baby dinosaur's life for the first year. Your book may include such things as:

> A newborn picture
>
> A weight chart
>
> List of favorite words
>
> Favorite foods
>
> Favorite toys
>
> Health record
>
> Foot and handprints
>
> Birth weight
>
> Name of baby
>
> Memories of the first Christmas
>
> List of other family members
>
> Other items of your choice

Share your finished baby album with your classmates.

HENRY AND THE DRAGON
by Eileen Christelow

Summary

Henry Rabbit has recurring bad dreams about a dragon living near his home. His dreams are fueled by a strange shadow that appears on his bedroom wall after dark. Finally, Henry uncovers the unlikely source of the shadow.

Vocabulary

1. fierce
2. tucked
3. twine
4. rustling
5. gasped
6. cast

Setting Reading Purpose

1. Henry's father reads him a bedtime story about dragons that prompts him to fear dragons lurking about after dark. What kinds of tricks can our minds play on us after dark?
2. How can Henry know for sure if a dragon is outside his house at night?

Questions During Reading

1. (literal) Why did Henry's father tell him that he should not worry about dragons? (They are only make-believe.)
2. (inferential) Why do Henry's parents look for the dragon since they have told him that it is only make-believe? (They want to calm his fears and prove dragons do not exist.)
3. (literal) How does Henry build his dragon trap? (He strings twine around the branches of the plants outside his home.)
4. (inferential) Why does Henry sleep better in his parents' bed? (He feels safe.)

Comprehension Skill Extenders

1. How is a shadow made? With a partner, create a silhouette with a light source. Trace the person's profile onto black paper with chalk. Cut out and mount it on white paper.
2. Is animal trapping a humane way to capture an animal? Why or why not? If you had to trap a troublesome animal, what kind of trap would you use? Describe and explain your choice.
3. Every good story has a problem and a solution. The solution is usually dependent upon the action of the characters. Identify the problem, character actions, and solution for *Henry and the Dragon*.

Curriculum Integration

What are some ways to prove shadow dragons are not dragons at all? Discuss possible ways of overcoming fears created by imagination.

HOW DROOFUS THE DRAGON LOST HIS HEAD
by Bill Peet

Summary
When the king discovers the presence of a dragon in his kingdom, he offers a reward for its head. Thanks to the love of a small boy and his family, Droofus loses his head in an unexpected way.

Vocabulary

1. dense	11. scurried	20. battered	29. sheepherder
2. weary	12. despair	21. sprawled	30. lances
3. gliding	13. brambles	22. pitiful	31. tomfoolery
4. pounce	14. looming	23. budge	32. festival
5. snatched	15. peer	24. tattered	33. splendorously
6. brute	16. scampering	25. seizing	34. elegant
7. clusters	17. stammered	26. pyramid	35. frolicsome
8. towering	18. fierce	27. jabbing	36. merriment
9. amazement	19. whirling	28. furrow	37. rafters
10. marvelous			

Setting Reading Purpose
1. Droofus is only 4 years old when he is separated from his family. He is very alone and hungry. Where does he first make his home?
2. How does Droofus the Dragon help the young boy and his family?

Questions During Reading
1. (literal) Who offers a reward for Droofus' head? (The king.)
2. (inferential) Why were the knights searching for a dragon in a cave with bones scattered in front of the entrance? (They figured that all dragons are meat eaters and would leave the bones from their meals by the cave somewhere.)
3. (literal) How was Droofus badly injured? (He was hurt in a big storm.)
4. (inferential) When did you first realize that Droofus was a kind dragon? (When he refused to eat the grasshopper.)

Comprehension Skill Extenders
1. Droofus ran into a terrible storm that caused him great injury. In reality, storms are responsible for many types of damage. List as many different types

of storms or dangerous weather conditions as you can. Choose one type to write a short paragraph about.

2. Droofus was a big help on the farm. If you were a modern-day crop farmer, what kinds of jobs would you have to do on the farm? List them. Would you like to be a farmer some day? Why or why not?

3. Saying that someone has "lost his head" is a figure of speech. Other figures of speech are: "it's raining cats and dogs," "there's a fork in the road," and "my, how time flies." Think of another figure of speech. Draw two pictures showing how it can sound figuratively and how it would look if we took it literally.

Example:

Curriculum Integration
The king borrows Droofus for the Grand Spring Festival. If you were the mayor of your town and responsible for planning a big town festival, what kind would you have? What would your festival celebrate? What events would you feature? Draw a poster advertising your festival.

NATE THE GREAT
AND THE STICKY CASE
by Marjorie Weinman Sharmat

Summary

Claude's Stegosaurus stamp mysteriously disappears, and it is up to Nate the Great and his dog Sludge to try to crack the case.

Vocabulary

1. detective
2. stegosaurus
3. swapping
4. museum
5. clue

Setting Reading Purpose

1. Why does Nate the Great call this a "sticky case"?
2. What clues does Nate the Great use to solve his case?

Questions During Reading

1. (literal) What is the name of Annie's dog? (Fang.)
2. (inferential) How did Nate the Great feel about Annie's dog? (He was scared by his big teeth.)
3. (literal) Where did Nate the Great go to find information about the Stegosaurus? (The museum.)
4. (creative) What else could you have done to solve the case more quickly? (Answers will vary.)

Comprehension Skill Extenders

1. If you were a zookeeper when dinosaurs were on earth, what kinds of animals might be in your zoo?
2. Tell why you think the dinosaurs died.
3. What animals do we have today that may look something like a dinosaur?

Curriculum Integration

Create a Dinosaur Family Album. Include at least five members of the dinosaur family. Use the album page form to gather your information and draw your pictures.

Dinosaur Family Album

by _____

This dinosaur is named

_____

Size _____

Weight _____

Foods it ate _____

_____

Where it lived _____

_____

How it defended itself _____

_____

_____

_____

Interesting facts _____

_____

_____

_____

Drawing of this dinosaur.

Why do you think it became extinct?

_____

_____

MY VISIT TO THE DINOSAURS
by Aliki

Summary

While visiting a museum of natural history, a young boy and his father and sister learn many interesting facts about dinosaurs.

Vocabulary

1. skeletons	5. embedded	9. nostrils	13. swift	17. defend
2. rods	6. paleontologists	10. powerful	14. armored	18. protected
3. plaster	7. carnivores	11. webbed	15. leathery	
4. fossils	8. herbivores	12. fierce	16. plated	

Setting Reading Purpose

1. Dinosaurs roamed the earth millions of years ago. How do scientists know what they looked like?
2. If you were a scientist who studied dinosaurs, what special title would you have?

Questions During Reading

1. (literal) Which dinosaur in the story was most capable of defending itself against Tyrannosaurus Rex? (Triceratops.)
2. (inferential) Which dinosaurs in the story were shown to be carnivorous? (Allosaurus, Ornitholestes, Ornithomimus, Tyrannosaurus.)
3. (literal) What special name is given to an animal that eats meat? (Carnivore.)
4. (inferential) Would you feel safer around a carnivorous or herbivorous dinosaur? Explain. (Herbivorous dinosaurs only eat plant life.)

Comprehension Skill Extenders

1. Choose five of your favorite dinosaurs from the story. Create a list of adjectives to describe each one. You may brainstorm ideas with a friend.
2. Create a dinosaur recipe using dinosaur meat instead of the traditional chicken or beef. List your ingredients. Then tell how the recipe would be prepared, cooked, and served.
3. Choose one of the dinosaurs from the story that was not labeled as a carnivore or herbivore and research to find out more about its eating habits.

Curriculum Integration

Follow these directions to create a sample of a fossil:

A. Fill a small box (like a checkbook box) half full of sand.
B. Place a cleaned bone (chicken bones work well) on the sand, then press it down just enough so it is halfway embedded in the sand.
C. Cover the bone (and some of the surrounding sand) with plaster of Paris.
D. Allow the plaster to dry. Remove the bone. Share your plaster fossil with your friends.

SARAH AND THE DRAGON

by Bruce Coville

Summary

Oakhorn, Sarah's unicorn friend, rescues her after she is kidnapped by a dragon and taken to his castle.

Vocabulary

1. unicorn
2. mane
3. pout
4. adventure
5. spell (noun)
6. cottage
7. blushed
8. swooped
9. spouting

Setting Reading Purpose

1. Sarah is captured by a fierce dragon in this story. How does she escape?
2. The dragon was not really just a dragon. What was the dragon turned into when he returned to his castle?

Questions During Reading

1. (literal) Who was Oakhorn? (Sarah's unicorn.)
2. (inferential) What is the most important thing that Sarah did to aid her safe return to her home? (She told Mrs. Bunjy to go and get Oakhorn to rescue her.)
3. (literal) After Aunt Mag cast her spell on Oakhorn, what happened to him? (He grew wings.)
4. (inferential) Why do you think Oakhorn felt Sarah ran away? (She had a quarrel with Oakhorn when she told him that he was grumpy and he told her that she was greedy.)

Comprehension Skill Extenders

1. Compare the problem, character actions, and solution found in *Sarah and the Dragon* to those found in *Henry and the Dragon* by Eileen Christelow. How are they different?
2. Find books that have dragons in them. Create a list of descriptive words for these dragons. Create an illustration of your own imaginary dragon.
3. Compare the dragons of writers' imaginations to the extinct dinosaurs of the past. If you could have one of these animals actually exist in a local zoo today, which one would you choose? Explain why this would be the best choice.

Curriculum Integration

Make a dragon out of clay or dough. After it is thoroughly dry, paint it with bright, bold colors. Spray it with a spray shellac to preserve its finish.

Dough Recipe

1 Cup Flour
1/2 Cup Salt
1/2 to 3/4 Cups Water
Knead thoroughly. Shape. Place on cookie sheet and bake for one hour at 225° F.

PATRICK'S DINOSAURS
by Carol Carrick

Summary

A Saturday visit to the zoo by Patrick and his big brother Hank prompts a conversation regarding dinosaurs. Patrick's imagination begins working overtime as he sees dinosaurs at every turn.

Vocabulary

1. brontosaurus
2. shrimpy
3. enormous
4. diplodocus
5. submarine
6. stegosaurus
7. plodded
8. triceratops
9. tyrannosaurus
10. prehistoric
11. tropical
12. dreadful
13. daggers

Setting Reading Purpose

1. Patrick and his older brother Hank visit the zoo. As they walk through the zoo, Hank tells Patrick about various types of dinosaurs. What effect do you think this discussion about dinosaurs will have on Patrick's imagination?
2. What information about dinosaurs might you learn from this story?

Questions During Reading

1. (literal) To what is the size of a brontosaurus compared? (Ten elephants.)
2. (inferential) What clue did Patrick use to conclude that the tyrannosaurus was a meat eater? (Dagger-like teeth.)
3. (literal) What physical feature allowed a diplodocus to stay under water? (Nose on top of its head.)
4. (inferential) What caused the dinosaurs to disappear from Patrick's imagination? (Hank explained that they had been gone for 60 million years.)

Comprehension Skill Extenders

1. Create a list of scientific facts about dinosaurs as given in the story.
2. If brontosaurus was the size of ten elephants, to what could you compare tyrannosaurus? Draw a picture of your comparison.
3. Do some additional research *and* use your imagination to create a fact and fiction book about dinosaurs.

Curriculum Integration

Use reference materials to locate facts about two other animals that have become extinct. Be sure to tell where they lived, what they ate, how long they lived, and why you believe they are extinct. Illustrate your report.

THE MAGICIAN AND THE DRAGON

by David McKee

Summary

When the king decides that his army is too fat and finds that a dragon has invaded his eastern kingdom, he decides to exercise his army with a dragon hunt.

Vocabulary

1. inspect	5. amused	9. fierce
2. bulged	6. interfere	10. squelched
3. dismissed	7. eager	11. mascot
4. challenge	8. keen	

Setting Reading Purpose

1. How does Melric the Magician save the friendly dragon from the king's army?
2. What prize does the king offer for finding the dragon?

Questions During Reading

1. (literal) Why was the king angry with the army? (They were too fat.)
2. (inferential) How were the soldiers and the dragon alike? (They all liked chocolate cake.)

3. (literal) What caused the people of the kingdom to run away from the dragon? (They thought that he would eat them.)

4. (inferential) How did Kra's advice help Melric? (When he related the story about the boy whose toys were everywhere but in the toy cupboard, he knew that the dragon would be hunted for everywhere but in the castle. Therefore, the castle would be the perfect place to hide the dragon.)

Comprehension Skill Extenders

1. If you had been in Melric's place, how else could you have helped the dragon?

2. There are two major problems in this story. What are the problems? How are they solved? Change the solution for one of the problems.

3. How are armies today different from the king's army? Prepare a list of the characteristics of each one.

Example:

The King's Army	An Army Today
1. Traveled on foot	1. Travels with trucks, tanks, etc.
2. Hunted dragons to lose weight	2. Exercises
3.	3.

Curriculum Integration

1. Go to the library and check out a book of magic tricks. Prepare a trick to share with your class.

2. Conduct some research on a famous magician to find out what his or her best trick was.

THERE'S NO SUCH THING AS A DRAGON

by Jack Kent

Summary

Billy Bixbee awoke one morning to find a dragon in his room. The more his mother denied its existence, the larger the dragon grew. An interesting turn of events takes place once the dragon's existence is acknowledged.

Vocabulary

   1. permitted   2. resist   3. insisted

Setting Reading Purpose

1. If you awoke with a dragon in your bedroom, your day would probably be quite different from a normal day. How does Billy's day change after the dragon arrives?
2. Is this dragon a friendly or a fierce dragon? How do you know?

Questions During Reading

1. (literal) Who ate Billy's pancakes? (The dragon.)
2. (inferential) Why do you believe that the dragon finally grew smaller again? (The family believed it was real.)
3. (literal) Why did the dragon take off down the street with the house on his back? (He smelled the fresh bread in the baker's truck and ran after it.)
4. (inferential) How do you know the dragon was happy to be recognized when Billy patted him on the head? (He wagged his tail and began to shrink.)

Comprehension Skill Extenders

1. When Billy first awoke and found the dragon, he told his mother about it but did not try to get rid of it. List at least five other things Billy could have done.
2. Design a house that would be movable but looks like a regular house. Draw a picture of your invention.
3. Create three or more headlines that might appear in a newspaper in Billy's town the day after the dragon takes the house for a ride.

Curriculum Integration

Put on your thinking cap and complete the chart on the reproducible student worksheet (p. 29). In each space write a word that begins with the letter to the left (a letter from the word DRAGONS) and that is a member of the category above (flower, food, country, animal, or name).

Dragon Acrostic

by _____

	flower	food	country	animal	name
D					
R					
A					
G					
O					
N					
S					

WE'RE BACK!
by Hudson Talbott

Summary

Rex and his dinosaur friends are magically transported to a New York City parade of the twentieth century. Trouble occurs, and they end up hiding in the Museum of Natural History.

Vocabulary

1. approaching	5. jolted	10. ceremony	15. extinct
2. test-marketing	6. utter	11. curious	16. publicity stunt
3. ultra	7. terrorizing	12. demonstration	17. Paleozoic Era
4. megavitamin	8. plunging	13. imitate	18. trilobite
	9. destiny	14. diorama	

Setting Reading Purpose

1. If dinosaurs came back to the earth for a visit today and walked through your city, what do you think would happen?
2. Which dinosaur was considered the most dangerous? Why?

Questions During Reading

1. (literal) What is the name of the ultra-megavitamin? (Brain Grain.)
2. (creative) Instead of using the ultra-megavitamin, Brain Grain, how could Vorb have gotten tyrannosaurus into his research school? (Answers will vary.)
3. (literal) How was Droofus badly injured? (He was hurt in a big storm.)
4. (creative) If you were Dr. Bleeb, how would you have protected the dinosaurs? (Answers will vary.)

Comprehension Skill Extenders

1. Write a short story for a local newspaper regarding the return of dinosaurs to earth in the twentieth century. Write it from the dinosaur's point of view. How have things changed?
2. Create a product that could have been popular during the time of the dinosaurs if man had been around then. Create a catalog or newspaper ad designed to sell your product.
3. Find a factual article about a dinosaur in an encyclopedia or other reference book. Write a summary of the important parts of the article.

Curriculum Integration

The American Museum of Natural History contains displays of animals that are now extinct. Pretend you are an architect and design a new museum. Sketch one room of the museum and its contents. The museum can be any type of museum. What would you name your museum? Where would it be located? (You may choose to create a diorama of your museum room.)

WHATEVER HAPPENED TO THE DINOSAURS?

by Bernard Most

Summary

A compilation of fanciful speculation regarding the question, "Whatever happened to the dinosaurs?"

Vocabulary

1. disguises 2. hibernating 3. shortage

Setting Reading Purpose

1. An age-old question follows us as we visit the library and read about dinosaurs. Whatever happened to the dinosaurs? What do scientists think happened to the dinosaurs to cause them to become extinct?
2. Using your wildest imagination, what do you think could have happened to the dinosaurs?

Questions During Reading

1. (literal) Who may have stolen the dinosaurs? (Pirates.)
2. (inferential) What would dinosaurs be doing at the North Pole? (Driving Santa's sleigh.)
3. (literal) What could dinosaurs do that is also done by bears? (Hibernate.)
4. (creative) If you went shopping for dinosaur food, what would you buy? (Answers will vary.)

Comprehension Skill Extenders

1. Illustrate your most imaginative idea of what could have happened to the dinosaurs. Add this to a classroom book.
2. Use reference materials to find information on ancestors of the dinosaurs. Create a brief, illustrated report on an ancestor of the dinosaurs.
3. If you were a scientist in charge of naming a newly discovered two-headed dinosaur, what would you name it? Explain your answer.

Curriculum Integration

1. When a dinosaur is unearthed by archaeologists, the bones are assembled to determine the skeletal composition of the animal. At this point, artists begin preparing a sketch of how the dinosaur may have looked. Create a drawing of your favorite dinosaur—bones only. Cut it apart and put it in a sandwich bag. Have a friend try to put your dinosaur together correctly.
2. How could dinosaurs and people live in harmony in the same land? What kinds of precautions would people have to take? How could a dinosaur become a family pet? Which dinosaurs would make the best pets? Why?

THE BRAGGIN' DRAGON
by Bill Martin Jr.

Summary

Written in "rap" form, this poetic adventure finds the Braggin' Dragon winning a backward spelling bee.

Vocabulary

1. thunderation	3. whiz-kid	5. glide	7. brag
2. toodle	4. dynamo	6. pogo	

Setting Reading Purpose

1. People sometimes brag about skills or talents they think they have. Have you ever bragged about doing something and then not done very well at it? What happens to the Braggin' Dragon at the Spelling Bee?
2. What does the Braggin' Dragon do to get to school on time?

Questions During Reading

1. (literal) How did the Braggin' Dragon spell the word "dragon" at the spelling bee? (NOGARD.)
2. (inferential) Why was Braggin' Dragon's mother upset with him "one mornin' early pearly"? (He wasn't getting ready for school. He was still asleep.)
3. (literal) Braggin' Dragon has many types of transportation. After the spelling bee, what does he ride as he celebrates? (Pogo.)
4. (critical) How would you describe the Braggin' Dragon? (Answers will vary.)

Comprehension Skill Extenders

1. The Braggin' Dragon sometimes uses pairs of rhyming words to describe nouns. (Nouns are words that name people, places, or things.) For example:
   1. <u>Sweet</u>, <u>beat</u> mornin'
   2. <u>Pearly</u>, <u>early</u> mornin'
   Make up your own rhyming pairs of words to describe morning. Since all mornings are not the same, create three or more sets of words.
2. Have your teacher help you find some music with a "rap" beat. Rap your favorite poem to the music. Let your class listen to your presentation.
3. The Braggin' Dragon used a pogo stick, roller skates, a bicycle, skis, a skateboard, and a motorbike for transportation. Without using a car, how else could he have gotten to and from school?

Curriculum Integration

Writing in rhyme requires us to write with a beat. Often we can find our beat by counting the number of syllables in a line.

     1   1   1   1   1 2   1

(8) And yeah, dear Mum, the lovin' cup

    1 1 1 1 1 1   1 1

(8) I give to you to cheer you up.

The rhyming lines should have similar counts—within one or two beats of each other.

Change the ending of the story. Begin your new ending after the part where the dragon gives the loving cup to his mom. Try to write the new ending using a rhyme with a similar beat pattern. "And now..."

THE TYRANNOSAURUS GAME
by Steven Kroll

Summary
Children amuse each other on a rainy school day by elaborating on a story starter about a tyrannosaurus crashing in on them at breakfast-time.

Vocabulary
1. plopped
2. tyrannosaurus
3. dashing
4. amusement park

Setting Reading Purpose
1. Jimmy tells a story about a dinosaur barging in on him at breakfast. How would you have changed this story starter?
2. If you were in Philip's place, how would you change the end of the story?

Questions During Reading
1. (literal) What game do the children in Jimmy's class play? (The story-starter game or the Tyrannosaurus Game.)
2. (inferential) Why did everyone else have to get off the bus when Jimmy and his friends arrived? (There wasn't enough room.)
3. (literal) Which one of the students drove a motorbike? (Denny.)
4. (inferential) Why couldn't the policemen find something as large as a tyrannosaurus? (It wrapped itself around the top of a very tall building and looked like a statue.)

Comprehension Skill Extenders
1. The author ends the story by allowing the dinosaur to disappear on the top of a building. How else could he have ended the story? Write a new ending for Philip.
2. Pretend that you are a new student in Jimmy's class. Write a section of the story that would fit between Debby and Rachel. Illustrate.
3. How would the story have been different if a pterodactyl joined Jimmy for breakfast? List three or more differences.

Curriculum Integration
Create a mural depicting the types of dinosaurs the class has learned something about. The background should depict the dinosaur's natural habitat.

OCTOBER

Mysteries and Magic

THE HOMEWORK CAPER

by Joan M. Lexau

Summary

Ken and Bill are neighbors who do everything together—even their homework. When Bill's homework mysteriously disappears, the boys try to piece together clues to find the missing paper.

Vocabulary

1. caper   2. arithmetic

Setting Reading Purpose

1. Teachers hear lots of excuses about why children have not done their homework on time. What is Bill's excuse for not having his homework done?
2. How does Ken help Bill solve the mystery surrounding the loss of his homework?

Questions During Reading

1. (literal) What kind of homework was Bill missing? (Arithmetic.)
2. (inferential) What kind of homes did Ken and Bill live in? (They lived in apartment buildings.)
3. (literal) What was the name of Ken's little sister? (Susan.)
4. (creative) Ken did not seem to realize how much Susan missed doing things with him. Even though she was much younger, she still wanted to join Bill and Ken. What are some things Ken could have done that would have made Susan feel better while allowing Ken and Bill the freedom they wanted from a little sister? (Answers will vary.)

Comprehension Skill Extenders

1. List as many words or complete phrases as you can find in the story that tell **where** the story took place. Then make a list of words or phrases that tell **when** the story took place.
2. Ken wanted Bill to try to do everything the same as he had done the day before to help him discover where his homework had gone. Draw a map that shows each place the boys travel as they try to make their day exactly the same as the day when the homework was lost.

Curriculum Integration

Creating a story with a good problem is important if the story is to be interesting to the reader. Losing homework is a real problem. Create a story in which the main character loses his or her homework and tries to tell a story about how it became lost. Make sure that the story has all the necessary ingredients—character, plot, setting, title.

One of the main characters in the story should help solve the problem of what happened to the homework. Be sure to tell how the teacher felt about the things that happened.

THE MYSTERY OF THE MISSING RED MITTEN

by Steven Kellogg

Summary

After Annie loses her fifth red mitten, an extensive search for the mitten begins. Children will delight in Kellogg's amusing ending.

Vocabulary

1. search
2. bloodhound

Setting Reading Purpose

1. We all know how hard it is sometimes to keep track of our mittens or gloves during the winter. It seems to be so easy to lose just one. Annie has lost five mittens this winter. Where does she finally find one of her lost mittens?
2. Annie finds some other things while she searches for her mitten. What else does she find?

Questions During Reading

1. (literal) Where does Annie search for her lost mitten? (She looks in places where she played in the morning.)
2. (inferential) Who is Oscar? (He is Annie's dog.)
3. (literal) How would a mouse family be able to use Annie's mitten? (As a sleeping bag.)
4. (inferential) In what season of the year does the story take place? (Winter.)

Comprehension Skill Extenders

1. Annie imagined that her mitten was being used in a couple of unusual ways—as a mouse's sleeping bag or as a head warmer for a baby hawk. Brainstorm with a friend to come up with as many unusual uses for a mitten as possible.
2. Annie dreamed of planting a mitten and growing a mitten tree. If you could plant an unusual type of tree, what type would you choose to plant? Why? Draw it.
3. Each of Kellogg's illustrations is a pencil sketch with a splash of red. Do a pencil sketch of a winter scene you can recall from memory. Use a splash of color for one particularly important item in the scene.

Curriculum Integration

Create a series of "mitten math" story problems that involve adding, subtracting, and money. Use note cards. Put the story problems on one side and the solutions on the back.

THE CASE OF THE CAT'S MEOW

by Crosby Bonsall

Summary

Four pint-sized private eyes try to solve the case of the missing cat. Snitch's beloved cat Mildred is missing, and a delightful surprise awaits the detective who solves the case.

Vocabulary

1. private eyes   2. porch   3. solved

Setting Reading Purpose

Private eyes come in all sizes and may be called upon to solve cases of all sizes as well.

1. If you were a child private eye searching for a missing cat, where would you look, and how would you try to lure the cat back home?
2. Snitch's cat gives the boys a real surprise. What do you think it could be?

Questions During Reading

1. (literal) What is Snitch afraid will happen? (His cat Mildred may be stolen.)
2. (inferential) Why didn't the alarm work on Mildred? (She jumped over the string.)
3. (inferential) Which brother is probably older, Snitch or Wizard? Why do you think so? (Wizard is quite a bit taller.)
4. (critical) Why do you think each of the boys wanted a kitten when they didn't seem to like Mildred very much? (Answers will vary.)

Comprehension Skill Extenders

1. Snitch and the other three boys eventually end up with cats for pets. If you could have any kind of animal in the world for a pet, what would you choose? Why would you choose it? How would you convince your parents to let you keep it?
2. There are several well-known comic strips using cats as characters. Use the Student Activity Worksheet (p. 41) to draw a comic strip using Mildred as the main character. Create an interesting title for your comic. Contribute your comic strip to a class comical cats book.
3. The trap that Wizard and his friends set up is similar to a Rube Goldberg invention. Do some research to find out who Rube Goldberg was and study his inventions. Be ready to explain Rube Goldberg to the class. You may wish to create a Rube Goldberg of your own.

Curriculum Integration

Crosby Bonsall chose to use only children and animals as main characters in his story. How would the story be different if adults were added? Write a part for a mother or a father in a major role in the story. How can they help solve Snitch's problem?

Comical Cats Contribution

by _____

Title

SIMON'S BOOK
by Henrik Drescher

Summary

A young boy becomes too drowsy to complete his story of Simon and the monster before going to bed. During the night, however, the pens and ink complete the job with delightful, imaginative results.

Vocabulary

1. drowsy	7. monstrous	13. collapsed
2. downy	8. predicament	14. relieved
3. stranded	9. thud	15. hermit crab
4. curious	10. crept	16. retired
5. shuffle	11. splatter	17. spacious
6. rustle	12. perched	18. amazement

Setting Reading Purpose

It is not unusual to begin writing a story one day and continue writing it the next day. It is odd, however, to wake up and find the story completely finished.
1. How did the young boy's story get finished while he slept?
2. What is one important word used in the book to describe the monster?

Questions During Reading

1. (literal) What did the monster do to Simon immediately after leaping toward him? (It gave him a big, sloppy kiss.)
2. (inferential) How many pens were involved in completing the story? (Two.)
3. (literal) What animal is the bottle of ink compared to? (A hermit crab.)
4. (creative) What is another way the pens and ink could have helped Simon? (Answers will vary.)

Comprehension Skill Extenders

1. The author of Simon's book uses several words interchangeably with the word "monster". List them, and add any others you think of.
2. Draw a picture of your favorite part of this story. Be prepared to explain why it is your favorite part.
3. The young boy in the story valued writing stories very much. Write about something you value doing. Tell why it is important to you.
4. How would the story have changed if the monster had been mean instead of friendly? Write a new ending having a fierce monster leap at Simon. Create one of the illustrations that would go with your new ending.

Curriculum Integration

Create a monster planter box to grow your very own friendly but monstrous plant. Save a milk carton. Cut it in half. Fill the bottom with small stones, then add black dirt.

Draw and color your most imaginative monster head and monster tail. Attach each to an end of the carton. Plant a couple of sunflower seeds. Water and place in a sunny area. Care for it regularly, and watch your monster plant begin to grow.

MY DOG AND THE KNOCK KNOCK MYSTERY

by David A. Adler

Summary

Jennie and her dog, My Dog, help Billy solve the mystery of why knocks on his door each night keep him awake.

Vocabulary

1. mysteries
2. porch
3. detective
4. solve
5. clues
6. fade

Setting Reading Purpose

1. Every mystery usually has a problem to solve. Judging from the title of the story, what kind of a problem will there be?
2. How does Jennie's dog My Dog help solve the mystery?

Questions During Reading

1. (literal) Why did Jennie name her dog My Dog? (She couldn't think of a good name for her dog.)
2. (creative) What would you have named Jennie's dog? Why? (Answers will vary.)
3. (literal) Why did Billy take the plants out of the living room? (They were hard to find when they needed to be watered because everything in the living room was green.)
4. (inferential) Why did Jennie's dog get sick? (She ate too many apples.)

Comprehension Skill Extenders

1. Jennie's dog played a big part in the story. If you were a detective and wanted a good watch dog, what kind of dog would you get? Do some research to find out which dogs would be the best. Complete the Watch Dog Qualification Chart on the Student Activity Worksheet (p. 45).
2. Because Billy's living room was all green, they could not find plants in it and were forced to get rid of them. What problems would he have if the living room was all white? All pink?
3. Billy and Jennie could have made good use of the apples My Dog ate. Create a new and original recipe that would use apples, and give your recipe a name.

Curriculum Integration

Design the house of your dreams. Draw either the floor plan or the outside of the structure. If you had to paint the inside and outside of the house the same color, what color would you choose? Support your choice.

WATCH DOG QUALIFICATION CHART

COMPILED BY _____

TYPE OF DOG	SIZE	TEMPERAMENT	SPECIAL QUALITIES

Watch Dog of my choice _____

_____

FOOTPRINTS IN THE REFRIGERATOR

by Selma and Pauline Boyd

Summary

A young girl becomes the family detective in order to solve the case of the mysterious footprints in the refrigerator.

Vocabulary

1. sofa	3. detective	5. pantry
2. goblins	4. magnifying glass	6. solved

Setting Reading Purpose

A detective has to search for clues that lead toward solving a mystery. What clues are used to solve the mystery of the footprints in the refrigerator? Who was making the footprints in the refrigerator?

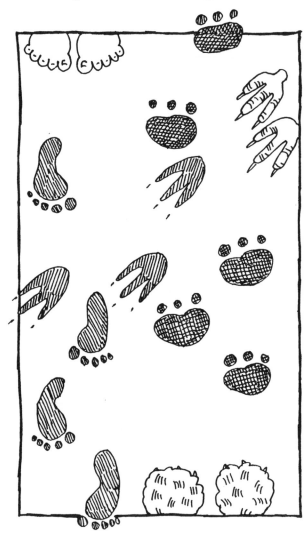

Questions During Reading

1. (literal) Who did the brother say might be responsible for creating the footprints? (Ghosts, goblins, or creatures from outer space.)
2. (inferential) Why did the brother feel his sister could not be a good detective? (She could not even find her homework, so she probably wouldn't be able to find anything else.)
3. (literal) What did the big sister use as bait to check and see if her little sister could climb? (Her sister's teddy bear.)
4. (critical) Although the little sister got the bear off the top of the refrigerator, why is it hard to believe she got her own cookies from the top of the refrigerator? (It would be hard not to knock over the cookie jar.)

Comprehension Skill Extenders

1. If you really wanted to become a detective, what kind of equipment do you think you would need to get your work done? See if the library has any information on detective work as a career choice. Try calling a detective agency for information.

2. Using an inkpad and the side of your hand, create your own mini-footprints down the edge of a piece of paper. Use the tip of your little finger for the toes. Then write your own story entitled "Footprints in the _____."

3. Pretend you are the author of this book. You run into a problem when you try to get your book published because someone else has already used the title *Footprints In The Refrigerator*. What new title would you want to use?

4. Compare the family in this story to your own family. How are they the same and different?

Curriculum Integration

Work in groups of six. Together, each group should decide on a story title and three or four story characters. Then each student should draw a scene from a story he or she imagines involving the given title and characters. (Work separately on your drawings.) After all drawings are completed, the group should decide on a sequence for their pictures. Then the group should cooperatively create a story and share it with the class.

STREGA NONA'S MAGIC LESSONS
by Tomie de Paola

Summary

Poor Bambolona, the baker's daughter, is having a hard time getting all the work done at the bakery, so Strega Nona invites her to stay and learn magic. When Big Anthony is fired from the bakery, he also causes disaster with the magic lessons.

Vocabulary

1. yeast
2. muttered
3. promptly
4. Signora
5. ancient
6. presto

Setting Reading Purpose

1. Big Anthony, as always, would like Strega Nona to teach him some magic. Strega Nona knows Big Anthony well enough to realize that he cannot handle magic. How does Big Anthony try to trick Strega Nona into teaching him magic?
2. Why does the baker's daughter Bambolona leave her job at her father's bakery?

Questions During Reading

1. (literal) What does Bambolona's father say to her when she tells him that she cannot get everything done? (Get up earlier.)
2. (inferential) How do you know that Strega Nona was never really turned into a toad? (The toad hopped past Big Anthony while Strega Nona was speaking with him.)
3. (inferential) Who did Big Anthony disguise himself as? (Antonia.)
4. (inferential) Why did Big Anthony dress up as Antonia? (Men could not become Stregas, and Big Anthony wanted to learn magic.)

Comprehension Skill Extenders

1. If you were opening a bakery in a new town and wanted to have a successful business, what are the things you would definitely want to have for sale? List all of the baked goods you would have.
2. If you were given magic powers for a brief period of time and could choose one object to change into something else, what would you change? What would you change it into? Explain your choice.
3. If you really wanted to disguise yourself so your family would not recognize you, how would you dress up? Draw a picture of your disguise and label the parts.

Curriculum Integration

Follow the thawing directions of a package of frozen dough. After it has thawed out, create a bread treat in an interesting shape. After the bread has baked, eat it with butter and/or sprinkle it with cinnamon sugar.

NATE THE GREAT
AND THE PHONY CLUE

by Marjorie Weinman Sharmat

Summary

This adventure story involves testing Nate the Great to see just how great his detective work is. Nate overcomes obstacles such as a phony clue to respond to an invitation to meet someone at three o'clock.

Vocabulary

1. phony   2. exercise   3. doorstep   4. sewer   5. invitation

Setting Reading Purpose

1. Nate the Great is not considered a great detective by all the children in his neighborhood. One of the children tries to prove he is not a great detective by setting up a phony clue as Nate the Great tries to solve a case. What is the phony clue?
2. How does Nate the Great finally solve the case of the phony clue?

Questions During Reading

1. (literal) What does Nate the Great do to the note he leaves for his mother? (Tears it into pieces and puts it back together again.)
2. (inferential) If Nate the Great could not read the phony clue because it was backward, what could he have used to help him read it? (A mirror.)
3. (literal) Who did not think Nate the Great was a great detective? (Finley.)
4. (inferential) Why did Nate the Great put the invitation in the water? (To see how it looked compared to the phony clue that he found in the sewer.)

Comprehension Skill Extenders

1. Rosamond uses the words "rip," "scratch," "shred," "cut," "tear," "slit," and "slash" to describe the ways Big Hex the cat can tear a piece of paper. What are some other words you could add to her list that all mean the same or nearly the same as "tear"? List as many as you can think of.
2. Nate the Great tells us that he has not seen the paper boat on the Pacific Ocean or the Atlantic Ocean. What kinds of boats might we see on either of these two oceans? Do some research to find out.

Curriculum Integration

Nate the Great saw the paper boat on a poster advertising Jamaica. The poster was designed to make people want to visit the country of Jamaica. Choose a country you think would be fun to visit. Find out what some of its main attractions are. Why would people wish to visit it? Design a poster advertising the country. Include pictures and factual information on your poster and make it as colorful as possible.

DO NOT OPEN
by Brinton Turkle

Summary

Miss Moody loves treasure hunting along the beach after a storm with her faithful cat Captain Kidd. Her treasure-hunting adventure takes on a new twist the day she finds the mysterious purple bottle that says, "Do not open!"

Vocabulary

1. repaid	5. furiously	9. gorgeous	13. astonished
2. banjo clock	6. crept	10. properly	14. snarled
3. blustered	7. stowed	11. stopper	15. vanished
4. chowder	8. driftwood	12. horrid	16. pounced

Setting Reading Purpose

1. Storms can make people feel uneasy or frightened. How do you feel during a terrible storm? Miss Moody, the main character in this story, looks at storms in an unusual way. How does she feel about them?

2. How are Captain Kidd and Miss Moody able to capture the mean, ugly genie from the bottle?

Questions During Reading

1. (literal) What was wrong with Miss Moody's handsome banjo clock? (It would not run.)
2. (inferential) What clues do you find in the story to prove that Captain Kidd hates storms? (He hid under the bed, and he would not eat the delicious chowder.)
3. (literal) What was wrong with the red rug? (One corner was missing.)
4. (critical) Where do you think the treasures that wash up on the beach come from? (Answers will vary.)

Comprehension Skill Extenders

1. Miss Moody finds some rather unusual treasures along the beach after the storm. What might the average person expect to find on the beach along the Pacific or Atlantic Coast? Use reference books to help compile an accurate list.
2. Put yourself in Miss Moody's place. You are holding the purple bottle with the stopper in it. Will you open the bottle or not? Explain your answer.
3. Every good story must have a problem. Miss Moody solved the problem in *Do Not Open* by tricking the genie in the bottle. In what other way could she have solved the problem? Write about it briefly and illustrate your idea.

Curriculum Integration

The real treasures of the ocean are its unusual forms of plant and animal life. Help to create pieces for a bulletin board entitled "TREASURES OF THE DEEP!" Draw and color fish and plants from the ocean that you find interesting and beautiful. Cut out each one and label. Pin your artwork on an appropriate place on the bulletin board.

GORKY RISES

by William Steig

Summary

Gorky concocts a potion which mysteriously allows him to fly. His travels end when he lands on Elephant Rock; this results in another mysterious happening.

Vocabulary

1. laboratory	11. glinted	21. bedazzled	31. plunge
2. tumbler	12. decanted	22. craning	32. bestir
3. talcum powder	13. solemnly	23. aeronauts	33. quiver
4. murky	14. sauntered	24. electrified	34. astride
5. paprika	15. immensely	25. flabbergasted	35. terrain
6. cognac	16. concocted	26. swarthy	36. scouring
7. vigorously	17. gruesome	27. frolic	37. crevice
8. witch hazel	18. impression	28. crimson	38. lumbering
9. ravished	19. astonished	29. aloft	39. doting
10. Attar of roses	20. bewildered	30. plummet	40. tremendous

Setting Reading Purpose

1. Gorky is a young frog who likes to experiment. He finally concocts a potion that causes something magical to happen. What does Gorky's magic bottle of potion do for him?
2. How does Gorky finally get back home after his unusual adventure?

Questions During Reading

1. (literal) What is the last ingredient that Gorky adds to his secret potion? (Attar of roses.)
2. (inferential) What convinced Gorky's parents that he was telling the truth about his adventure? (Elephant Rock was missing.)
3. (literal) How did Gorky get back down from the sky? (He let the liquid drip from the bottle one drop at a time and slowly sank down.)
4. (inferential) How long was Gorky gone on his adventure? (One day.)

Comprehension Skill Extenders

1. Gorky seemed to sense the necessary ingredients for his magic potion. If you were going to create a magic potion, what would you use for ingredients? List them. What would you want your potion to do for you?
2. Gorky enjoyed doing silly antics in space. He stuck his arms in his armpits. He

crossed his eyes, clicked his heels, and wiggled his hips. What kinds of things would you do to show off if you were flying over your school playground during recess?

3. From the context clues found on the second page of the story, can you figure out what "decanted" means? Write its meaning, then use it in another sentence.

Curriculum Integration

The first real fright Gorky had while in flight came from the fierce-looking kites. Pretend you are the master kite-maker for your state. Using construction paper, tissue paper, crayons, and water colors, design a beautiful kite that will make people feel good when they see it.

TWO-TON SECRET

by Mary Blont Christian

Summary

When the police are unable to find the thief of a construction-site bulldozer, Deke and Snitch, undercover kid detectives, take the case. In an unexpected turn of events, they solve the crime.

Vocabulary

1. associate	6. detectives	11. phony	16. flatbed
2. expenses	7. frontage	12. bulldozer	17. serial numbers
3. skidded	8. mutter	13. suspect	18. drooped
4. construction	9. undercover	14. ignitions	19. evidence
5. hard hat	10. disguises	15. spark plugs	20. metal detector

Setting Reading Purpose

1. The thieves in this story steal large construction machines called bulldozers. Even after the construction site owner has fenced in the area, a machine is stolen. How could a thief steal something so large?
2. What clues do Deke and Snitch use to help them solve the crime of the stolen bulldozers?

Questions During Reading

1. (literal) How did Mr. Drake plan to make his machinery easier to spot if it was stolen? (He was going to paint it green with pink polka dots.)
2. (inferential) When the boys got to the construction site, why did Snitch begin throwing powder on everything in sight? (He was checking for fingerprints.)
3. (literal) Where did the thieves take the stolen bulldozer? (They didn't take it anywhere. It was buried.)
4. (creative) If you were one of the undercover kids, what type of a disguise could you find quickly at your home? (Answers will vary.)

Comprehension Skill Extenders

1. Choose either Deke or Snitch and create a list of words that describe the character. Compare this character with a real person you know personally. Tell the ways the two are alike and different.
2. It is important for an author to make the story "come alive" for the reader. The reader should be able to see and hear what is happening in the story through the author's descriptions. Which words in the story helped the story become

more real to you? List them. How could the author have made the story more real?

3. Write five sentences you feel tell the most important things to happen in the story. After you make your list, compare it with a friend's list. Cooperatively try to come up with a sentence that tells the main idea of the story.

Curriculum Integration

Deke and Snitch are a pair. They work together and seem to enjoy being together. Cake and ice cream seem to be another common pair — things that seem to fit well together. List as many things as you can think of that are pairs. Choose your favorite pair to illustrate. Put together a class book entitled "We Go Together."

WANDA AND THE BUMBLY WIZARD

by James Flora

Summary

Wanda's life changes when she rescues a wizard who has forgotten how to "magic himself up a cliff" that he has fallen down. Although most of his magic does not work quite as planned, the journey to the castle of the queen will amuse and amaze readers.

Vocabulary

1. canvas	6. perched	11. orphan	16. monstrous
2. wedged	7. strutted	12. coaxed	17. bleating
3. fetch	8. bumble	13. scruffy	18. astounded
4. twine	9. squishy	14. canal	19. confounded
5. wizard	10. confessed	15. quivering	

Setting Reading Purpose

1. Wanda is an orphan on her way to visit the queen when she meets a wizard. How do Wanda and the wizard get to the castle?
2. What kinds of magic tricks does the wizard perform on the way to the castle?

Questions During Reading

1. (literal) What was wrong with the tent the wizard created? (It had holes in it.)
2. (inferential) What would have happened to Wanda if the rope did not pull her back when she fell off the bed? (She would have smashed into the ground.)
3. (literal) What did the giant do to the wizard's magic rope? (He ate it.)
4. (creative) Why do you think the giant was so mean? (Answers will vary.)

Comprehension Skill Extenders

1. The wizard caused the bed to fly so he and Wanda would not have to walk to the castle. If you could cause something of yours to fly you to school each day, what would it be and why?
2. Wizard fuzz is certainly powerful stuff. In fact, it can even make things disappear. It cannot, however, bring something back once it has disappeared. If you had enough magic fuzz to make one thing disappear forever, what would you sprinkle it on? Explain your choice. Remember, you can never get it back again!
3. Many objects that we have today have old-fashioned names that have been used to describe them in the past. Some objects have two names that mean the same

thing. Make a list of each.

Examples:

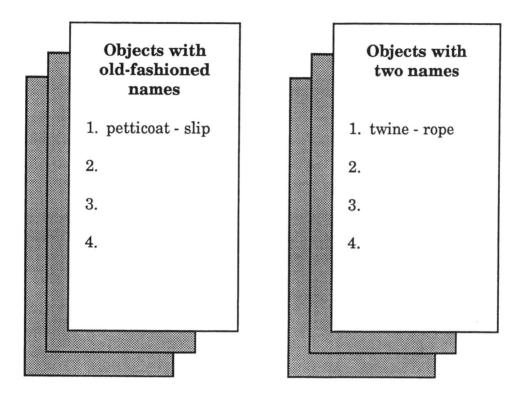

Objects with old-fashioned names

1. petticoat - slip

2.

3.

4.

Objects with two names

1. twine - rope

2.

3.

4.

Curriculum Integration

Bumbly Wizard was able to transform the mean and nasty wizard into a kind and considerate one with a little help from Wanda. Human beings know that people who behave in mean and unkind ways usually do so because they do not feel very good about themselves. If you wanted someone who was very unpleasant to you and your friends to become a nicer person, what are some things you could do? List them.

LIANG AND THE MAGIC PAINTBRUSH

by Demi

Summary

An intriguing old Chinese folktale in which a poor young boy named Liang is given a paintbrush capable of creating paintings that come to life.

Vocabulary

1. China	6. appeared	11. merchants	16. imprisoned
2. gathering	7. phoenix	12. crane	17. enormous
3. reeds	8. immediately	13. emperor	18. python
4. glared	9. lanterns	14. bound	19. keeled
5. beggar	10. marketplace	15. furious	

Setting Reading Purpose

1. This story has an intriguing title and cover design. After studying these for a few minutes, what do you think the paintbrush will be able to do?
2. Magic makes it possible to change things. How do you think the magic paintbrush will change Liang's life?

Questions During Reading

1. (literal) How did Liang get the magic paintbrush? (An old man on a Phoenix placed it in his hand as he slept.)
2. (inferential) What is a Phoenix? (A large, imaginary bird.)
3. (literal) What happened after Liang painted deer with his new paintbrush? (They came to life.)
4. (inferential) How did the greedy emperor find out about Liang's magic paintbrush? (He painted a crane for a man that accidentally came to life. Once the man saw the magic, he told others, who told others, until the emperor finally heard.)

Comprehension Skill Extenders

1. Put yourself in Liang's place. Take a piece of drawing paper. Fold it in half and then in half again. You now have four sections to your paper. Paint something in each section you would want to create if you had a magic paintbrush. Write a title for each picture with a dark crayon.
2. The story is somewhat unfinished. Create an ending for the story that explains what happened to Liang.

3. Research to find out how paint is made. Experiment with color. Using only yellow, red, and blue paint, how many new colors can you create by mixing small amounts of each?

Curriculum Integration

What if paintbrushes did not exist? How could artists create painted pictures? Without using a paintbrush, paint a picture. Do not use your fingers!

AUNT EATER LOVES A MYSTERY
by Doug Cushman

Summary
Aunt Eater loves to read and solve mysteries. She finally gets a chance to solve a real mystery.

Vocabulary

1. anteater	4. chilly	7. boiler	10. laundromat	13. muttered
2. decided	5. conductor	8. jewel	11. embarrassed	14. alley
3. porter	6. butler	9. stammered	12. cozy	15. tingled

Setting Reading Purpose
1. Aunt Eater the anteater loves to read mysteries. Her problem is that she feels mysteries are happening everywhere around her. What kind of mysteries does she get involved with?
2. How does Aunt Eater solve the cat mystery?

Questions During Reading
1. (literal) What did Aunt Eater find in her suitcase on the train ride to visit her sister Eliza? (Tools.)
2. (inferential) What caused the spooky shadow to appear on the wall at Eliza's party? (Alfred the butler was raising his tray and glass.)
3. (literal) What food did Sam the cat not like to eat? (Fish.)
4. (inferential) Why does Aunt Eater seem to be so suspicious of others? (They remind her of characters in her mystery stories.)

Comprehension Skill Extenders
1. Become a detective yourself. Find out more about the author of this book. You may write to him in care of his publishing company Harper and Row. Decide on six to eight good questions to ask in your letter. Be sure to tell him something about yourself.
2. Sam the cat did not enjoy eating fish. Find out more about what cats do eat. Write a few sentences about caring for and feeding a cat. Share this information with the class.
3. Aunt Eater has a good time with many other animals in this story. Do research to find out which of the following would not be friendly to an anteater in the wild: bear, rhinoceros, elephant, goat, pig, fox, squirrel, cat, dog, and alligator.

Curriculum Integration
Pretend you are a small-town news reporter. You have just received a call from a neighbor of Aunt Eater who would like you to do a feature story about the anteater. Plan an interview that you could enact with another student. Have a friend play the part of Aunt Eater. (Make sure your friend has read or heard the story.) Conduct your interview for members of the class to observe.

NOVEMBER

Giants and Monsters

THERE'S A MONSTER UNDER MY BED

by James Howe

Summary

Simon imagines many monsters under his bed after he agrees he no longer needs a nightlight. He is surprised to find something alive under his bed.

Vocabulary

1. mattress   2. slimy   3. drooly   4. munch

Setting Reading Purpose

1. When it is late at night and very dark in our rooms, we sometimes imagine all sorts of things. What does Simon really find under his bed?
2. How do Simon and his younger brother finally get over their fear of monsters?

Questions During Reading

1. (literal) What is the name of Simon's younger brother? (Alex.)
2. (inferential) Why do you think Simon really asked his brother Alex to sleep with him in his room? (So neither Simon nor Alex would be so scared.)
3. (literal) Why did Simon get rid of his nightlight? (He told his mom he was too old for a nightlight.)
4. (creative) What does the last picture suggest to you? (Answers will vary.)

Comprehension Skill Extenders

1. Simon fears he will find unpleasant things under his bed. If you looked under each of the beds at your house, what would you find? List the items and compare your list to a friend's list.
2. Design a monster trap that will fit under a typical bed. Write a brief description of the way it works.
3. Make a list of twenty-five words that would help you take your mind off being scared because they would help you think of happy things.

Curriculum Integration

It is important to have a good imagination even though our mind may dream up some rather scary ideas at times. List five people from the past or present you feel had or have a good imagination. Explain why you feel each person is unique.

THE VERY WORST MONSTER
by Pat Hutchins

Summary
Older sister Hazel wants to prove to her family that she is a worse monster than her baby brother Billy. She surprises her family by doing just that.

Vocabulary
1. fangs   2. competition   3. definitely

Setting Reading Purpose
1. A truly bad monster must look frightening as well as do frightening things. What does Billy do to prove he is the worst monster?
2. What does Hazel do to get rid of her baby brother Billy?

Questions During Reading
1. (literal) What did Billy Monster's dad want him to be when he grew up? (The worst monster in the world.)
2. (inferential) What did the postman do after Billy scared him? (He climbed a tree.)
3. (inferential) What did Billy do to help him win the "Worst Monster Baby in the World" competition? (He tried to eat the judge.)
4. (inferential) After Hazel gave her brother away, what did her parents say? ("You must be the worst monster in the world.")

Comprehension Skill Extenders

1. Hazel cannot get her family to listen to her. They seem to give all their attention to baby Billy. If you were in Hazel's place, what would you do to get your parents' attention?

2. Reread the parts in the story that describe Billy and Hazel. Compare them by size, age, appearance, actions, likes and dislikes, etc. Make a list of how Billy and Hazel are alike and how they are different.

Example:

Ways in Which Billy and Hazel are Alike	Ways in Which Billy and Hazel are Different
both have pointed ears	

3. Create a third child for the Monster Family. Draw him or her and tell about the child's important characteristics.

Curriculum Integration

Billy Monster had "wonderful" fangs. Using reference books, create a list of animals living today that have fangs. Find out how fang-like teeth benefit animals. Write a short paragraph or two about an animal with fangs, telling how the fangs are helpful.

THE GIANT'S TOE

by Brock Cole

Summary

One day while hoeing cabbages, a giant cuts off his toe. The toe, in turn, springs to life and causes the giant enormous problems. The giant is upset until the toe saves the day.

Vocabulary

1. ought
2. kindling
3. greedy
4. aroma
5. velvet
6. foul
7. bellowed

Setting Reading Purpose

1. *The Giant's Toe* is similar to a fairy tale. It also talks about things that happen in another fairy tale. What other fairy tale does it remind you of?
2. What happens to the giant's toe after he cuts if off?

Questions During Reading

1. (literal) How does the giant cut his toe off? (He whacks it with the hoe.)
2. (inferential) How do you think Jack got to the giant's house? (He probably climbed the bean stalk.)
3. (literal) Why didn't the giant have his toe sewn back on? (It might prick him.)
4. (creative) Was it a good idea to keep the toe? Why or why not? (Answers will vary.)

Comprehension Skill Extenders

1. The giant thought of two possible ways to reattach his

toe before it changed into a small person. He thought about gluing it or sewing it back on. In what other ways could he have reattached his toe? List four ideas. Choose your favorite and tell why you feel it is a good idea.

2. The giant tried to get rid of the changed toe by eating it in a pie and throwing it to China. Neither idea worked. How would you get rid of the toe?

3. The story of the giant's toe is lighthearted fun. He does not really suffer from cutting off his toe. However, millions of people in the United States suffer injury from serious home accidents. Do research to find out what kind of accidents occur in people's homes each year. List several of them and outline a safety plan to help deal with one of them.

Curriculum Integration

The Giant's Toe uses characters found in *Jack and the Beanstalk*. Create another giant story using different characters from another fairy tale. You may choose to use the *Big Bad Wolf*, the *Three Little Pigs, Goldilocks, Sleeping Beauty, Rapunzel, The Seven Dwarfs, Cinderella, The Handsome Prince*, or any other fairy tale characters. How does the character help the giant solve a problem or create a problem for the giant? Illustrate one part of your story.

THE SELFISH GIANT
by Oscar Wilde

Summary

Spring refuses to return to the garden of the selfish giant after he forbids the children to play in it. The giant's heart is softened by the hug and kiss of a small boy.

Vocabulary

1. delicate	4. determined	7. prosecuted	10. bitterly	13. marvelous
2. bore	5. gruff	8. linnet	11. companion	14. hastened
3. ogre	6. trespassers	9. casement	12. feeble	

Setting Reading Purpose

1. The children loved playing in the garden by the castle of the selfish giant. Why did the children suddenly stop playing there?
2. What happened to the beautiful garden when the children no longer played there?

Questions During Reading

1. (literal) Who was the giant visiting during his seven-year absence from his castle? (The Cornish Ogre.)
2. (inferential) Why did the little boy give the giant a hug and a kiss? (The giant helped him by lifting him up into the tree.)
3. (creative) Why is the season of winter chosen as a punishment for the giant? (Answers will vary.)
4. (literal) What did the frost do to the garden? (It painted all the trees silver.)

Comprehension Skill Extenders

1. We never actually see the beautiful garden of the Selfish Giant. We do know, however, that the plants had almost human-like qualities. Using water colors, create a beautiful, colorful garden. Personalize your plants by giving each of them faces. Be sure to give your painting a title.
2. The giant was punished for not allowing the children to play in his garden. Was his punishment fair? Why or why not? What other type of punishment would you give the giant?
3. Use twenty-five words to describe the selfish giant. Use ten words to describe the children.

Curriculum Integration

When we think about walls, like the walls around the selfish giant's gardens, we often think of something unpleasant. While this story is purely imaginary, there are some real walls that have been built by countries that have great historical importance. Do research to find information about an important wall in history. Tell why it was built, where it was built, who built it, when it was built, and what it was built of.

THE MYSTERIOUS GIANT OF BARLETTA
by Tomie de Paola

Summary
This is an Italian folktale about the mysterious giant statue found in the town of Barletta. This story tells how the mysterious giant saved the town from an invading army.

Vocabulary

1. convent	4. Adriatic	7. pedestal	10. strode	13. bellowed
2. hailed	5. destroying	8. miracle	11. lieutenants	
3. bargain	6. Holy Mass	9. scurried	12. dumbstruck	

Setting Reading Purpose
1. The town of Barletta has a famous giant statue in its town square. How does the statue save the town from the invading army?
2. The statue is given an onion by Zia Concetta. Why does she give an onion to a statue?

Questions During Reading
1. (literal) In English, what did Zia Concetta say to the statue each night? (Good-night, Big One.)
2. (inferential) What did Zia Concetta mean when she handed the giant the onion and said, "Buena fortuna"? (Good fortune.)
3. (literal) How did the statue use the onion? (He held it close to his eyes to make them water as though he were crying.)
4. (inferential) At the end of the story, how did the giant show Zia Concetta that he understood her? (He winked.)

Comprehension Skill Extenders
1. Do research to find out about men and women famous in your state. Design a statue that would be appropriate in your town. Draw it and tell why you chose the person you did.
2. Barletta was a small Italian town—quiet and peaceful. List small towns in your area of the state. Then list the benefits of living in a small town.
3. The Mysterious Giant of Barletta did not have a name, and no one really knew how he got to Barletta. Create a story that explains who he is and how he got to the town square in Barletta.

Curriculum Integration
Towns certainly are not the only places where statues honoring people or events can be built. If you were in charge of building a statue or designing a plaque for your school honoring someone or something, whom or what would you choose? Sketch your statue or plaque, or mold one of them from clay. Explain why your person or event deserves special recognition.

THE FRANKENBAGEL MONSTER
by Daniel Pinkwater

Summary

A lighthearted spoof on fresh bagels that always go stale just before they are ready to be eaten. Harold Frankenbagel, local bagel-maker, creates an unruly bagel monster.

Vocabulary

1. popular	7. command	13. accounts	19. stale
2. bagel	8. ghastly	14. supernatural	20. tamper
3. miniature	9. lurching	15. lumbers	21. violent
4. unnatural	10. populace	16. renegade	22. nutritious
5. incredible	11. precisely	17. lox	23. civilization
6. immense	12. various	18. incredibly	

Setting Reading Purpose

1. Harold Frankenbagel, owner of Bagel Master, strives to create the world's best bagels. He travels all over the state tasting bagels and examining them. What are the electronic bageloids that he talks about?
2. How was the bagel monster finally stopped?

Questions During Reading

1. (literal) Why did Harold Frankenbagel create the bagel monster? (He wanted to be the greatest bagel-maker in history.)
2. (inferential) Why was the bageloid monster referred to as a renegade? (He was acting without permission from his inventor and did things that other bagels would not do.)
3. (literal) How does the bagel monster get his power? (He gets it from a bag of bright blue garlic.)
4. (inferential) What does Harold Frankenbagel consider to be his greatest creation? (The Glimville Bagelunculus.)

Comprehension Skill Extenders

1. Harold Frankenbagel desires to create the world's greatest bagel. If you were a wonderfully creative bagel-maker, what would be your most unusual bagel creation?
2. Create a list of twenty uses for a plain bagel.
3. Professor Sir Arnold Von Sweeney has studied several cases of strange events where food has gone mad. Some of those cases involved Night-Stalking Celery,

Vampire Squash, and Chopped Liver. Create a newspaper article that describes a problem created by unruly food. Illustrate your story.

Curriculum Integration

Daniel Pinkwater has created his own lighthearted Murphy's Law. "Bagels always go stale just before we're ready to eat them." Identify other problems that seem to regularly occur that are slightly annoying. Compile a list of five or six ideas, then develop your own original monster character around one of them.

Example:
   Idea: "The water in the shower always turns cold just after you have applied the shampoo to your hair."
   Character: Cold Water Clem
   Description: Tall and thin, Clem always wears a shower cap pulled over his right eye. He wears transparent boots and speaks with a trickling laugh. Clem loves to munch on bread and water and delights in watching goose pimples form on people's arms.

SOUP FOR SUPPER

by Phyllis Root

Summary

A wee, small woman had only a garden for company. Then Giant Rumbleton pulled up all her vegetables for his supper soup.

Vocabulary

1. wee	4. mulch	6. enormous	9. shrieked	12. bundled
2. slugs	5. mulberry	7. thunderous	10. bellowed	13. fiercely
3. rutabagas	bush	8. scurrying	11. pelting	14. ladle

Setting Reading Purpose

1. The title of the story suggests that someone would like soup for supper. Find out who actually has soup for supper.
2. The wee small woman in the story becomes very upset when the giant begins to steal her vegetables. What are some of the names she calls the giant?

Questions During Reading

1. (literal) The giant is able to smell things very well. Which sense is his weakest sense? (His sense of sight.)
2. (inferential) Why didn't the giant take the vegetables back from the wee small woman once she gathered them in her apron? (Answers will vary.)
3. (literal) Although the wee small woman did not need the giant's help to replant her garden, why did she let him stay? (She wanted a friend.)
4. (inferential) Why couldn't the giant stay at the home of the wee small woman? (There was not enough room for him.)

Comprehension Skill Extenders

1. Compare Giant Rumbleton to the selfish giant in Oscar Wilde's book, *The Selfish Giant*. How are they alike? Different?
2. The wee small woman and Giant Rumbleton create a delicious soup together. Pretend that you are the chef at an expensive, well-known restaurant. A very important customer has requested that you make a special soup for his wife's birthday party. He has asked that the soup have at least two types of vegetables in it and one must be green. Write the recipe for the soup you will make, and tell how it needs to be prepared. Don't forget to include what you will name your special soup.
3. Long ago, people had to plant gardens to raise their own foods to live on. If you knew your family would have to live off the foods from your garden for one year, what would you plant? Draw your garden and label the different rows of plants.

Curriculum Integration

At the end of the story, the author has included the song the giant was singing, "The Soup Song." Create a fourth verse for this song.

NO MORE MONSTERS FOR ME

by Peggy Parish

Summary

An unusual replacement is found when Minneapolis Simpkin is not permitted to have a pet (an *I Can Read* book).

Vocabulary

1. tadpole
2. Minneapolis Simpkin

Setting Reading Purpose

1. Minneapolis Simpkin really wants a pet. However, her mother has told her that she may not have one. On her long walk she finds something to substitute for a pet. What does she bring home?
2. Minn's mom finally allows her to get a pet at the pet store. What kind of pet does she get?

Questions During Reading

1. (literal) What did Minneapolis Simpkin's mom tell her that monsters will eat? (Pickles.)
2. (inferential) Why couldn't Minneapolis bring her mother a second apple from the basement? (She said that the monster would eat all of them.)
3. (literal) What kind of pet did Minneapolis Simpkin's mother buy for herself? (A kitten.)
4. (creative) Do you think that Minneapolis Simpkin really brought home a monster? Why or why not? (Answers will vary.)

Comprehension Skill Extenders

1. Minneapolis Simpkin's mom told her that monsters eat pickles. What do you think they eat? Create a menu that you would find in a restaurant that sells food only to monsters; include breakfast foods, lunches, and dinners. Be sure to put the name of your restaurant on your menu.
2. If your mom would not allow you to have any pets at your house but you could have anything else that you wanted, what would you choose? Why?
3. Draw the scariest monster you can think of. Tell about the type of character it would be.

Curriculum Integration

Prepare a story problem for the classroom "Monster Math" book. Draw and cut out a monster. Write the problem on the front of the monster and the answer on the back. Give it to your teacher when you have finished.

Example: Once upon a time Matilda Monster was going to the store to buy pork rinds for her three baby "monsterlettes." She had $5 in her purse. Pork rinds cost $4.75 for twelve. How much money would she get back from her $5?

Answer: $5.00
                        -4.75
                        $ .25   Matilda Monster would get 25¢ back.

MAYBE A MONSTER

by Martha Alexander

Summary

When a young boy sets a trap, he decides to make a cage to accommodate the monster he might catch. His cage far exceeds his catch, causing young readers to giggle with delight.

Vocabulary

1. enormous   2. protected   3. slingshot

Setting Reading Purpose

1. Building a trap is an exciting experience when it is done in a way not harmful to the animal being trapped. But what if you caught something in your trap that you were not expecting—maybe a monster? What kind of cage does the young boy build in case he has to catch a monster?
2. How does he protect himself when he goes to get his catch?

Questions During Reading

1. (literal) Why does the young trapper take his water pistol to the trap? (To put out the monster's fire.)
2. (inferential) How does the young trapper build his trap? (He digs a hole and covers it with branches.)
3. (literal) What does the young trapper catch? (A rabbit.)
4. (inferential) What does the young trapper make his cage of? (Wooden board.)

Comprehension Skill Extenders

1. If you wanted to safely set a trap that would not be harmful to animals or anything else, what kind of trap would you create? Draw it and write an explanation of how it works.
2. The trapper caught a rabbit in his trap. Create a new ending for the story in which the young boy catches something else.
3. If you were approaching a trap and did not know what you would find inside, how would you protect yourself? Think of things you could find around your home that you could use. List them. Draw a picture of yourself with your protective equipment.

Curriculum Integration

The young trapper has no real idea what he will catch. His trap is built to accommodate a monster that he pictures in his mind. After you have determined what you will catch, make a model of a cage you have designed specifically for your catch. Use a shoe box or similar box as the basis for your creation. Provide a detailed written explanation of the features of your cage.

MY MAMA SAYS THERE AREN'T ANY ZOMBIES, GHOSTS, VAMPIRES, CREATURES, DEMONS, MONSTERS, FIENDS, GOBLINS OR THINGS

by Judith Viorst

Summary

In *My Mama Says There Aren't Any Zombies, Ghosts, Vampires, Creatures, Demons, Monsters, Fiends, Goblins or Things*, Nick isn't so sure that all the things that go bump in the night may not, indeed, exist. Mama says that they don't, but she's been known to be wrong before.

Vocabulary

1. cozy	3. fiend	5. zombie	7. demon	9. goblin
2. positively	4. drizzle	6. clonking	8. slinking	10. brussels sprouts

Setting Reading Purpose

1. Sometimes when it is dark, we let our imaginations run away with us. What kinds of things does Nick imagine are trying to get him?
2. Of course, we all know that people make mistakes. It's part of being human. What kinds of mistakes has Nick's mom made?

Questions During Reading

1. (literal) Whose skates were really on the sidewalk when Nick got blamed? (They were Anthony's.)
2. (inferential) Once Nick's mom did not give him enough money to buy a yo-yo. How much more money did he need? (6 cents.)
3. (literal) What food does Nick believe boys and girls eat in goblin-y lands? (Brussels sprouts.)
4. (inferential) Why doesn't Nick believe his mother about the fiends, ghosts, and zombies? (He doesn't believe her because she has made other mistakes.)

Comprehension Skill Extenders

1. Make a list of all the different types of monsters you can think of. Tell which one you feel is the most frightening and why.
2. Nick's mom has made some mistakes any mom could have made. Tell about a mistake you remember your mom making. Share your memory with the class.
3. Carefully choose seven words to best describe your mom or another member of your family. Tell about qualities your mom or another family member has that you admire. Put your words into a poem.

Curriculum Integration

Becoming a parent is a job for which no formal training or education is required. If the country created a new law that said that all people who wanted to become parents would have to go to parenting school for one year, what kinds of classes do you think they should be required to take? List ten or more courses you think parents should have. Describe one class in detail.

ABIYOYO
by Pete Seeger

Summary

Once upon a time a young boy played a howling ukelele, and his magician father made things disappear. The people of the village forced them to leave until they performed a heroic act.

Vocabulary

1. ukelele   2. ostracized   3. precious   4. possessions   5. staggered

Setting Reading Purpose

1. Abiyoyo is based on a South African lullaby and folk story about a frightening giant named Abiyoyo. How do the young ukelele-playing boy and his father help get rid of this giant?
2. What does the giant like to eat?

Questions During Reading

1. (literal) What did the old people of the village tell stories about? (A frightening giant named Abiyoyo.)
2. (inferential) Why didn't the children of the village believe the stories about giants and Abiyoyo? (No one had seen Abiyoyo.)
3. (literal) Why did the giant lie down? (He had become tired from dancing.)
4. (creative) Why did the giant need to be lying down for his father's magic to work? (Answers will vary).

Comprehension Skill Extenders

1. This story is based on a folktale which Pete Seeger declares needs to be changed in some way each time it is told. Decide on a change you would like to make in the story. Tell your story to a friend or a small group of friends.
2. The boy's mother is not a character in the story. Add a mother. Tell about why she, too, would be ostracized from the village.
3. The song about Abiyoyo is very simple. Create a more complicated version of the song.

Curriculum Integration

Folktales are meant to be told from generation to generation. Each time one is told the story changes slightly. Do research to find another folktale that is interesting to you. Find out what country the tale originates from. Practice telling the story until you can share it with a group from memory. You may choose to use some of the story illustrations as you tell it.

HARALD AND THE GIANT KNIGHT
by Donald Carrick

Summary

When knights threaten to hold their spring training on Harald's farm, his family is forced into action to save their home.

Vocabulary

1. baron	9. mock	17. boundary	25. loom
2. eel	10. strutted	18. spits	26. clamor
3. passageways	11. ruined	19. plunder	27. bewildered
4. wondrous	12. harvest	20. thrash	28. groped
5. chambers	13. arena	21. reeds	29. shambles
6. tunics	14. transformed	22. thicket	30. milled
7. jousts	15. lances	23. ravine	31. dumbfounded
8. tournaments	16. tended	24. mounted	

Setting Reading Purpose

1. Harald always wanted to be a knight. While delivering baskets to the baron's castle, he watched the large, scarred men with envy. What changes Harald's mind about wanting to become a knight?
2. How does Harald's family create a giant scary enough to frighten the Baron's brave knights?

Questions During Reading

1. (literal) Name the members of Harald's family. (His mother, his father, Helga, and Walter.)
2. (inferential) Why did Harald say that the knights behaved like thieves? (Harald watched them ruin the farmland, steal livestock, and plunder the farms.)
3. (literal) How did Helga help with the construction of the giant? (Helga made a cape for the knight.)
4. (inferential) From what material was the giant woven? (The giant was woven from reeds.)

Comprehension Skill Extenders

1. Life during the Middle Ages was quite different from our lives today. If you lived during the Middle Ages, how would your life be different? (Use reference books to help you. The details in Carrick's drawings are very accurate and will help you get information.)

2. If Harald's father had not been a basket weaver, how else could the family have created a giant knight? Describe what you would do, and draw a picture of your knight.

3. Harald was inventive and courageous. Which one would you rather be? Tell why.

Curriculum Integration

You are the proud owner of a medieval European castle. It has been given to you by a great-great aunt whom you have never met. In order to be able to afford to keep the castle, you will need to earn money by giving castle tours. Design a brochure to advertise your castle by taking a piece of paper and folding it into thirds. On each section include a different bit of information about the castle. Some of the things you may wish to include in your brochure are:

1. Pictures of the castle.
2. History of the castle.
3. Price of the tour.
4. Days and times of tours.
5. Famous people who have stayed at the castle.
6. Directions to get to the castle.
7. Names of the current castle owners.

Include your own ideas as well.

A LITTLE TOUCH OF MONSTER
by Emily Lampert

Summary

Parker, a scrumptious little darling of a boy, is fed up with not having his wishes considered when decisions that affect him are made. As a result, he comes down with "a little touch of monster."

Vocabulary

1. unannounced	6. interfered	11. aghast	16. triumphantly
2. unspeakable	7. midair	12. eldest	17. scone
3. scrumptious	8. preferred	13. expectant	
4. passersby	9. menacing	14. reluctantly	
5. definitely	10. anxiously	15. hastily	

Setting Reading Purpose

1. Parker is the youngest of three children. He is polite, pleasant, and well-liked by everyone. Why does he decide to turn into a misbehaving monster child?
2. What is Parker's favorite color?

Questions During Reading

1. (literal) What did Parker not want to be when his sisters played house? (The baby.)
2. (inferential) Why didn't Parker want his chocolate scone? (He had so much chocolate to eat that he didn't want any more.)
3. (literal) Who was the first one to think that Parker needed to have more attention? (His father.)
4. (inferential) How did Parker show his family he no longer wanted to be a monster? (He told them that monsters eat chocolate all the time and that he didn't care for any.)

Comprehension Skill Extenders

1. Parker's family was able to cure their own little monster by paying more attention to him. What if someone in your family came down with "a little touch of monster"? Write a cure your parents could follow to prevent "monsteritis."
2. If you were in Parker's place and no one ever seemed to listen to you, what would you do to get your family's attention?
3. If you had a little touch of monster, what are some of the naughty things you might do? List them.

Curriculum Integration

Parker's favorite color is blue. Take a survey of everyone in your classroom. Ask each what his or her favorite color is. Record your data on the reproducible student worksheet (p. 81). Fill in a space for each color given as a favorite with crayon in the proper color to create a colorful bar graph.

Surveyor _____

Class _____

Date _____

Favorite Colors

Red																			
Blue																			
Yellow																			
Green																			
Purple																			
Orange																			
Pink																			
Black																			
White																			
Other																			

BIG ANTHONY AND THE MAGIC RING
by Tomie de Paola

Summary

Although Big Anthony knows he should not use Strega Nona's magic ring, he finds himself in trouble when he attempts to turn himself into a handsome man.

Vocabulary

1. perk	4. wane	7. rummaged	10. convent	13. budge
2. tarantella	5. Eastertide	8. strolled	11. priest	14. cypress
3. elegant	6. ragazzo	9. fountain	12. Amore	15. flagon

Setting Reading Purpose

1. Big Anthony feels tired and lazy. His head is fuzzy. Strega Nona tells him that he has spring fever. How does Big Anthony get rid of spring fever?
2. Every time Big Anthony tries to do Strega Nona's magic, something goes wrong. What happens to him when he borrows Strega Nona's magic ring?

Questions During Reading

1. (literal) What happened to Strega Nona when she used the magic ring? (She turned into a beautiful lady in elegant clothes.)
2. (inferential) Why didn't the ladies leave Big Anthony alone when he wanted to quit dancing? (They thought he was so handsome, they all fell in love with him.)
3. (literal) What did Strega Nona do to help Big Anthony get the ring off his finger? (She rubbed olive oil on his finger.)
4. (creative) If you were able to borrow the magic ring on the sly, what would you do? Why? (Answers will vary.)

Comprehensive Skill Extenders

1. Strega Nona and Big Anthony sometimes speak in Italian. Find out how to say something to another person in a different language. Check the library for information on Spanish, German, or another language.
2. Big Anthony had a bad case of spring fever. In the spring, many changes take place. List as many changes as you can think of that occur in the spring.
3. The answer is, "A Magic Ring." What are some questions that could be answered this way? List at least five.

Curriculum Integration

Big Anthony and Strega Nona come from a small village in Italy. Write a short paragraph about one of its cities, and draw a picture of something you would find there. Tell one way your city is different from the Italian city and one way it is the same.

DECEMBER

Christmas and Food For Thought

THE POLAR EXPRESS
by Chris Van Allsburg

Summary

In the wee hours of Christmas Eve, a boy rides the Polar Express to the North Pole and receives a reindeer's bell as a gift. Although he loses the bell, it mysteriously reappears under his tree on Christmas Day to jingle a joyous sound heard only by believers.

Vocabulary

1. conductor
2. nougat
3. flickered
4. barren
5. pressed (through the crowd)
6. lurch

Setting Reading Purpose

On Christmas Eve a boy rides the Polar Express to the North Pole and is chosen to receive the first gift of Christmas. What gift does he ask of Santa?

Questions During Reading

1. (literal) What does the boy discover when he looks for the cause of the sound of hissing steam? (The train called the Polar Express causes the sound.)
2. (inferential) Who can ride on the Polar Express? (Children who believe in Santa Claus may ride.)
3. (literal) How did the boy lose the bell? (He put it in his bathrobe pocket and there was a hole in it.)
4. (inferential) Who can hear the music of the reindeer bells? (Anyone who believes in Santa.)

Comprehension Skill Extenders

1. The conductor told time using a pocket watch. Why do we have mostly wrist watches today with very few pocket watches?
2. The method of transportation chosen for this story is a train. Why do you feel the author chose a train rather than a plane or a car?
3. If you were in the boy's place, what gift would you have chosen and why?

Curriculum Integration

There are several different names for Santa Claus throughout the world. Do research to find five of them. List them and give the most important characteristics about each one.

THE CHRISTMAS DAY KITTEN

by James Herriot

Summary

James Herriot, a country vet, tells the beautiful true story of a wonderful Christmas surprise at the Pickering house.

Vocabulary

1. Basset hounds	5. obviously	10. apologetically	15. festive
2. timid	6. occasion	11. surrounding	16. sedate
3. tabby	7. nibbling	12. staggered	17. retriever
4. upright	8. daintily	13. bedraggled	18. unimpressed
	9. flitting	14. ornate	

Setting Reading Purpose

Mrs. Pickering has three Basset hounds that she cares for very much. Sometimes she is visited by a stray cat that she has named Debbie. What does she say is her best Christmas present ever?

Questions During Reading

1. (literal) What is James Herriot's job? (He is a veterinarian.)
2. (inferential) Describe Mrs. Pickering. (Possible answers: plump, pleasant, kind, caring, wealthy.)
3. (literal) What does Debbie do when she wants to give herself a little treat? (She goes to the sitting room and watches the fire.)
4. (inferential) Why do you think Debbie died? (Answers will vary.)

Comprehension Skill Extenders

1. This story is a true story (nonfiction). If you have pets, you may have a true story of your own to write. If you do not have a true story of your own, change something about *The Christmas Day Kitten* to make it a story that would not be as sad.
2. Find out as much as you can about the work a veterinarian does. Then list three reasons why you would enjoy the job and three reasons why you would not enjoy it.
3. Explain why you believe the author chose the title *The Christmas Day Kitten* for his story.

Curriculum Integration

Choose a type of cat and do some research on it. Use the reproducible student worksheet (p. 87) to record your information. Draw a detailed picture of the kind of cat you have chosen. Write one sentence of factual information about the cat underneath the picture. Put all the pictures together to form a class "Cat Album." (Each student may want to choose a different type of cat.)

Cat Researcher
and Illustrator _____

Name of Cat: _____

Special Information: _____

_____

_____

_____

SANTA'S CRASH-BANG CHRISTMAS

by Steven Kroll

Summary

Santa wishes he were home on Christmas Eve when a series of near-catastrophes happens as he delivers gifts.

Vocabulary

1. sleigh	3. collapsed	5. hinges	7. blundered
2. perfectly	4. chandelier	6. umbrella	8. teetered

Setting Reading Purpose

Santa has some problems at the Sylvesters' house. He falls out of his sleigh, forgets his handkerchief and his watch, and knocks over the Christmas tree. What kind of a surprise does he find in his bag?

Questions During Reading

1. (literal) Why isn't Gerald, the elf, happy he has come along with Santa? (He thinks it is too much work.)
2. (creative) Why did the sofa collapse? (It may have been ready to break, or maybe Santa was too heavy for it.)
3. (literal) How did Santa get back out of the Sylvesters' house? (He went out the window.)
4. (inferential) Why does Santa wish he were home? (Everything seems to be going wrong.)

Comprehension Skill Extenders

1. What do you think Santa should have done with the polar bear? Draw a picture of your solution to Santa's problem.
2. Santa is not having a very good day. Write about something that happened to you when you were having a very bad day.
3. It appears that Santa can use some help with all the deliveries he needs to make. Write an ad for the "Help Wanted" section of the newspaper in an attempt to get some help for Santa. Look over this section in your local paper before beginning.

Curriculum Integration

The Polar Bear is an animal that lives in the arctic region of the world. Research and compare the polar bear to the brown bear, the grizzly bear, and the panda bear. Use the reproducible student worksheet for recording this information.

Name or Type of Bear:

_____

Average Size: _____

Usual Color:_____

Foods it Eats: _____

_____

Places Found: _____

_____

Lifespan: _____

Drawing Of Bear In Its Natural Habitat

Name or Type of Bear:

_____

Average Size: _____

Usual Color:_____

Foods it Eats: _____

_____

Places Found: _____

_____

Lifespan: _____

Drawing Of Bear In Its Natural Habitat

Name or Type of Bear:

_____

Average Size: _____

Usual Color:_____

Foods it Eats: _____

_____

Places Found: _____

_____

Lifespan: _____

Drawing Of Bear In Its Natural Habitat

Name or Type of Bear:

_____

Average Size: _____

Usual Color:_____

Foods it Eats: _____

_____

Places Found: _____

_____

Lifespan: _____

Drawing Of Bear In Its Natural Habitat

MORRIS'S DISAPPEARING BAG
by Rosemary Wells

Summary

When Morris's older brothers and sisters share Christmas gifts, Morris feels left out. Morris, however, finds one remaining box under the Christmas tree that contains a disappearing bag and changes the way everyone feels about sharing with Morris.

Vocabulary

1. chemistry	4. test tubes	7. overlooked
2. chemicals	5. goalie	8. disappearing
3. acids	6. invented	9. recognize

Setting Reading Purpose

1. Morris likes the bear he got for Christmas until his brothers and sisters refuse to share their toys with him. How does Morris get his brothers and sisters to let him use their Christmas gifts?
2. What do you think a disappearing bag might be?

Questions During Reading

1. (literal) Who is the youngest member of the rabbit family? (Morris.)
2. (inferential) Why wouldn't Morris eat his dinner? (He was upset because no one wanted to share with him.)
3. (inferential) How did Morris's mother and father try to make him feel better? (His mother offered to help make a hat for his bear, and his father offered to take Morris and his bear for a walk.)
4. (creative) How did Morris know that the box had a disappearing bag in it if he could not see it? (Answers will vary.)

Comprehension Skill Extenders

1. Think of ten ways to use a disappearing bag. List them.
2. Morris found an unusual gift in the last box under the tree. Tell how the story would have changed if there had been something else in the box.
3. *Morris's Disappearing Bag* uses an apostrophe to show that the bag belongs to Morris. Practice writing sentences using apostrophes to show possession.

       Examples:
          1. The_____ coat was very warm.
                 girls   girls'   girl's

2. Several _____ roamed the street.

   dogs   dogs'   dog's

3. The _____ books were all scattered on
the floor.

   childrens   childrens'   children's

4. It's not _____ job to clean the living room.

   Johns   Johns'   John's

5. The lightning struck the _____ tricycle.

   childs   childs'   child's

Curriculum Integration

Write a television commercial that could be used during the Christmas season
to advertise your new product – the "Disappearing Bag."

Your commercial should take between 30 seconds to one minute to act out. It
should tell people clearly and in a persuasive way why they want to buy the
product and how the product is used. It should also tell where the product is
available.

Gather your necessary props, and perform your commercial for the class.

91

MERRY CHRISTMAS, STREGA NONA

by Tomie de Paola

Summary
Big Anthony decides to give Strega Nona a big surprise for Christmas – a surprise Christmas party.

Vocabulary
1. advent
2. dawdle
3. codfish
4. periwinkles
5. Venice

Setting Reading Purpose
1. Strega Nona spends weeks getting ready for Christmas and the feast she makes for all the people in town. What does Big Anthony give Strega Nona for Christmas?
2. What do the words "Strega Nona" mean?

Questions During Reading
1. (literal) Why can't Bambolona help Strega Nona get ready for Christmas? (She has to help her father at the bakery.)
2. (inferential) Why does Big Anthony want Strega Nona to use her magic? (Then he will not have to work so hard.)
3. (literal) Why couldn't Strega Nona give her Christmas feast? (Big Anthony forgot the supplies from her list and forgot to soak the cod.)
4. (inferential) What do you think Strega Nona means when she says, "Christmas has a magic of its own"? (Answers will vary.)

Comprehension Skill Extenders
1. *Merry Christmas, Strega Nona* takes place in Italy. Research to find out more about the way Italians celebrate Christmas.
2. Strega Nona had certain important decorations she used during Christmas such as the advent wreath, lemon blossoms, and periwinkles. When you are grown up and have a home of your own, what decorations will you always want to use at Christmas? Explain your choices.
3. List ten words that come to mind when you think of Christmas. Ask a friend to do the same thing. When you are both finished, compare your lists. How are they alike? Why are there some differences?

Curriculum Integration

Strega Nona always has the companionship of Bambolona and Big Anthony. Create a new character that Tomie de Paola could use in his Strega Nona stories. Write as many details as possible about the character. Would he or she have any special talents? How would he or she help Strega Nona? Draw a picture of the character you have created.

93

THE GIANT JAM SANDWICH

by John Vernon Lord

Summary

When Itching Down develops a wasp problem, the town people prepare a giant jam sandwich trap. A lighthearted, humorous rhyming tale.

Vocabulary

1. pate
2. nuisance
3. suggestion
4. yeast
5. sprout
6. hitched
7. spades

Setting Reading Purpose

1. When the village of Itching Down is suddenly plagued by 4 million wasps, the people of the village have to act quickly. How are they finally able to get rid of the wasps?
2. What is special about the way the story is written?

Questions During Reading

1. (literal) Who finally offers a suggestion for getting rid of the wasps? (The barber.)
2. (inferential) Why did the birds carry off the giant jam sandwich? (Birds love to eat insects.)
3. (literal) Where was the giant jam sandwich built? (In Farmer Seed's field.)
4. (creative) What other foods could the villagers have baked that would have attracted the wasps? (Answers will vary.)

Comprehension Skill Extenders

1. The author tells us that three wasps escaped, but no one knows where they went. Create a story telling about the wasps after they left Itching Down.
2. When the flying machines took the top slice of bread up into the air, a flying tractor was used. Create another unusual flying machine. Draw a detailed picture of the machine and explain what its advantages would be.
3. If the village had been unable to use food as a trap to get rid of the wasps, how else might they have gotten rid of them? Describe your plan for the villagers.

Curriculum Integration

Insects such as locusts have created serious problems for people throughout history. Do research to find out more information about insect plagues. Share your information with the class.

Research for information about an insect you are curious about. Then create a brief rhyme or poem about it and illustrate it.

For example:

> I've always been quite fascinated by the fly,
> From every hot dish to dessert, it gives food a try,
> When Mom asked me to taste broccoli, I said, "Not I."

MRS. PIG'S BULK BUY

by Mary Rayner

Summary

Mrs. Pig's family of piglets has a favorite food, ketchup, until she makes it a little too plentiful.

Vocabulary

1. piglets	4. trotters	7. crimson	10. larder
2. enormous	5. sloshed	8. snuffled	11. doling
3. cuffing	6. tureen	9. marmalade	

Setting Reading Purpose

1. The piglets absolutely love ketchup on everything no matter what Mrs. Pig cooks. What happens to the pigs because they want to eat so much ketchup?
2. How does Mrs. Pig feel about her pigs asking for ketchup all the time?

Questions During Reading

1. (literal) What is Mother Pig's bulk buy? (Ketchup.)
2. (inferential) How do the piglets feel about ketchup sandwiches in their lunch? (They throw them away.)
3. (literal) What did the piglets have for breakfast with their ketchup? (Cereal.)
4. (inferential) Why did Mother Pig give the pigs so much ketchup? (She wanted to make them tired of eating it so they wouldn't want to put it on all their foods.)

Comprehension Skill Extenders

1. Create two lists. On one list put all the foods you think might taste good with ketchup on them. On the other list, name all the foods you think would taste terrible with ketchup on them. Illustrate one example from each list.
2. Do research to find out what ingredients are in an average bottle of ketchup. Write a paragraph of information about its nutritional value.
3. Find ten words in the story to which you could add a suffix.
     Example: smile + ing = smiling
   Then write a sentence for each of the ten words with their suffixes.

Curriculum Integration

Try your hand at some animal alliteration. Decide on one consonant letter from the alphabet. Think of as many words as you can that begin with your letter. Decide on an animal that also begins with your chosen consonant letter.
Now put together an alliterative sentence that tells about your animal in some way. In alliteration, each word in the sentence begins with the same letter.
     Example: Fred's friendly, frisky, funny fish flipped forward falling fast.
Illustrate your sentence.

LOVE FROM AUNT BETTY

by Nancy Winslow Parker

Summary

When Charlie receives a special chocolate fudge cake recipe from his Aunt Betty, he decides to try it right away. The strange, unexpected results seem to be due to the unusual added ingredients.

Vocabulary

1. Carpathian   2. Transylvania   3. gypsy   4. pantry

Setting Reading Purpose

Charlie eagerly mixes together the ingredients needed for Aunt Betty's chocolate fudge cake. How does it look when it first comes out of the oven?

Questions During Reading

1. (literal) What unusual ingredients were in the cake? (Cobwebs and dried tree toads.)
2. (inferential) Who did the recipe for the chocolate fudge cake originally come from? (An aged gypsy woman who lived in the mountains.)
3. (literal) Who sent Charlie the recipe? (His Aunt Betty.)
4. (literal) What happened when Charlie stuck the monster with a large knife? (It exploded and gave Charlie a beautiful cake and other goodies.)

Comprehension Skill Extenders

1. Uncle Clyde is mentioned in the story as the man who brought the recipe and the tree toads from Transylvania. Describe the kind of person you think Uncle Clyde would have been. Then compare Clyde to one of the uncles.
2. Charlie likes to bake. Therefore, his aunt has sent him a recipe with some interesting ingredients. What kinds of hobbies do you have? What are some great gifts relatives could send you that would not cost much?
3. Do some research to find out if Transylvania exists or has ever existed. Write a short paragraph on your findings.

Curriculum Integration

Use the reproducible student worksheet (p. 97) to create your own delicious-sounding dessert recipe. Tell how to mix the ingredients and how to bake them. Draw a picture of your finished dessert. Make sure your dessert will contain a surprise when it is opened!

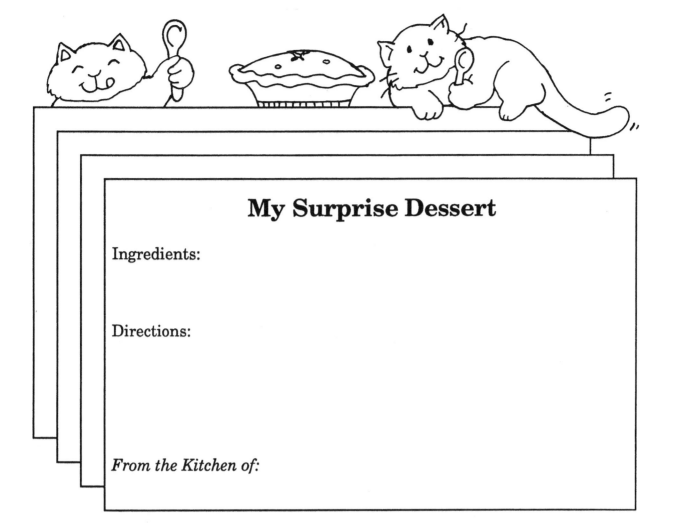

My Surprise Dessert

Ingredients:

Directions:

From the Kitchen of:

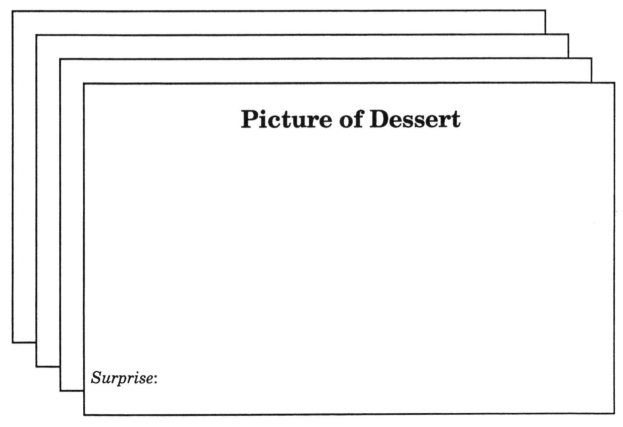

Picture of Dessert

Surprise:

JAM

by Margaret Mahy

Summary

Mr. and Mrs. Castle and their three small children live in a white house with a large yard. When Mrs. Castle goes to work as a scientist, Mr. Castle stays home to care for the children and the house and to make jam. Of course you can never have too much of a good thing. Or can you? (A true story.)

Vocabulary

1. cottages	5. anxious
2. atomic scientist	6. challenge
3. electronic	7. Picasso
4. sunspots	8. devoted

Setting Reading Purpose

1. Mr. and Mrs. Castle and their three children have a great deal of jam to eat when Mr. Castle becomes a great jam-maker and homemaker. What happens when the very last jar of jam is eaten?
2. How has eating all of Mr. Castle's jam affected his family?

Questions During Reading

1. (literal) What kind of work did Mrs. Castle do? (She was an atomic scientist.)
2. (creative) When all of Mr. Castle's jam was eaten and he heard the soft thud and saw the plums on the tree again, what do you suppose he did? (Answers will vary.)
3. (literal) In what two ways was the jam useful as well as delicious? (For mending the leaking roof and putting tile back in place.)
4. (inferential) Why did Mr. Castle say the children were more like cottages? (They were small.)

Comprehension Skill Extenders

1. Mr. Castle used his jam in a couple of creative ways. Think of at least two other uses for his jam. Why would his jam be good for your new ideas?
2. Mr. Castle made a lot of jam. If your mom or dad made a lot of one food product, what would you want them to make? Explain your choice.
3. Find out what it would cost to buy a jar of jam. Next, find a good jam recipe for the same type of jam you have priced. Price the ingredients in the jam, and

find out what it would cost to make (1) if you bought your fruit and (2) if you grew your own fruit. Record your information and compare results.

Example:

A. Store-bought Jam	B. Jam made from purchased ingredients	C. Jam using your own fruit and purchasing other ingredients

Curriculum Integration

Take a survey of your classmates to determine their favorite types of jam. After you have gathered all your information, use graph paper to create a graph of your results. If possible, survey the adults in the school to discover their favorite jams. Graph these results separately. Compare the two graphs.

ARTHUR'S CHRISTMAS

by Marc Brown

Summary

Arthur's concern for Santa helps teach his younger sister D.W. a valuable lesson about giving.

Vocabulary

1. long johns
2. seriously
3. subgum chow goo
4. whiff

Setting Reading Purpose

Arthur is shopping for a special gift for Santa Claus. He wants it to be something Santa will really like. What does he finally decide to give Santa for Christmas?

Questions During Reading

1. (literal) Why did Buster tell Santa to be careful coming down the chimney at his house? (His parents always forget to put out the fire.)
2. (inferential) Why is Arthur upset there is so little time left before Christmas Eve? (He has not found the right gift for Santa.)

3. (inferential) Why do you think Arthur put shoes on the pizza he made for Santa? (He heard the waitress yell out Santa's order and say "...put a pair of shoes on it..." He didn't know she meant the order should be rushed.)

4. (inferential) Who really wrote the letter to Arthur on Christmas? Why do you think so? (D.W.; reasons will vary.)

Comprehension Skill Extenders

1. D.W. tells Arthur to get the same gift for everyone as she does. How do you feel about this idea? Why do you feel the way you do?

2. Marc Brown hides the names of his two sons Tolon and Tucker in the illustrations of most of his books. See if you can find them in *Arthur's Christmas*.

3. Santa is on TV eating a product called "Papa Piper's Pickled Peppers." What other foods can you create with names that sound like tongue twisters? How about "Greg's Great Green Gooey Gum"? Create four. Then take a piece of drawing paper and fold it in half and then in half again to divide into four sections. Put one new product in each section of the paper by listing its name and illustrating the way it would look.

Curriculum Integration

Arthur knows one of life's great truths – it is better to give than to receive. Our parents give us important advice to live by such as:

1. Be sure to eat your vegetables.
2. Look both ways before crossing the street.
3. Treat other people the way you want to be treated.

Think of some important advice your parents have given you. Make a poster to help advertise this advice to others.

ANGELINA'S CHRISTMAS

by Katherine Holabird

Summary

Angelina and her family help brighten Christmas for the elderly, retired postman. He, in turn, shares his story and his Santa Clause expertise.

Vocabulary

1. rehearse
2. pavement
3. cottages
4. disappeared
5. glimpsed
6. pleasure
7. *Nutcracker Suite*

Setting Reading Purpose

Angelina wants everyone to be happy during the Christmas season. What does she do for Mr. Bell so he is not lonely?

Questions During Reading

1. (literal) What kind of Christmas surprise did Angelina and her family prepare for Mr. Bell? (A basket of cookies, pies, and fruits and a Christmas tree.)
2. (inferential) Why did Henry give Mr. Bell his cookie? (He wanted to give his cookie to Santa Claus, and he thought that Mr. Bell was Santa Claus.)
3. (literal) What kind of special presentation did Angelina's school have at Christmas? (They danced the *Nutcracker Suite*.)
4. (literal) Why wasn't Mr. Bell a postman any longer? (He was too old.)

Comprehension Skill Extenders

1. The story of Angelina's Christmas is told from a mouse's point of view. Pretend you are a mouse in the corner of your classroom. Describe your day from the time the students arrive until they leave.

2. Angelina is concerned about Mr. Bell because he is old and alone. What are some things you and your classmates could do to help elderly people in the area? Brainstorm a list of possible ideas. Plan with your teacher to do one of them.

3. The cottages in Angelina's village were all decorated in a similar way. If you could have the families on your street decorate their houses for Christmas in the same way, how would they look? Draw a picture of your block as it would look decorated.

Curriculum Integration

Angelina's storybook mouse family has a miniature home that is very much like a person's home. Using a shoe box or other small box, create a room in miniature that would be suitable for Angelina's family.

Use construction paper to create furniture that will stand up. Decorate the walls in the box.

THE CHRISTMAS CAT
by Efner T. Holmes

Summary

This is the heartwarming story of a little lost cat united with a loving family on Christmas Eve. It highlights love shown for all living things and the special magic of Christmas.

Vocabulary

1. gusting	6. territory	11. elusive	16. suet
2. huddled	7. crèche	12. enveloping	17. lulled
3. piteously	8. hovered	13. beckoned	18. fleeting
4. deserted	9. flickered	14. serenely	
5. in vain	10. forbidding	15. mangled	

Setting Reading Purpose

1. (literal) What kinds of ornaments are Jason and Nate making for the Christmas tree? (Gingerbread animal cookies.)
2. (inferential) Who was the man in the forest feeding the animals? (Jason and Nate's father.)
3. (literal) Why was the cat in the forest with the wild animals? (Her family had moved from their home while she was gone. She was looking for a new home.)
4. (inferential) *The Christmas Cat* shares some of the special traditions of Jason and Nate's family. What are they? (The crèche, gingerbread ornaments, feeding the forest animals on Christmas eve, filling stockings hung by the fireplace.)

Comprehension Skill Extenders

1. We oftentimes use animal names in expressing our feelings. Some common animal expressions are:

1. Eats like a pig.	4. Quick as a bunny.	7. Sly as a fox.
2. Stubborn as a mule.	5. Butterflies in my stomach.	8. Quiet as a mouse.
3. Wise as an owl.	6. Eyes like a hawk.	9. Horsing around.

   Choose two of your favorites from the list above or think of two of your own. Then explain what they mean and illustrate them.
2. Share some of the traditions that are part of your home during the Christmas season. What is your favorite tradition? Why?
3. What do you think the theme of this story is?

Curriculum Integration

Compare the story of *The Christmas Cat* to the story *The Christmas Day Kitten* by James Herriot. How are they alike and different? Which one do you prefer? Why?

GREGORY THE TERRIBLE EATER
by Mitchell Sharmat

Summary

Gregory, the young goat, has peculiar eating habits his parents are trying to break. He prefers people food to junk food until he learns to balance the two. He also learns that trying new foods can be a great experience if not overdone.

Vocabulary

1. average
2. certainly
3. fussy
4. revolting
5. munching
6. terrible
7. horrible
8. develop
9. stomachache

Setting Reading Purpose

Gregory likes people food even though he is a goat. His parents finally teach him to eat junk such as shoelaces and rubber heels. What was Gregory's problem after he learned to eat junk?

Questions During Reading

1. (literal) Why did Gregory get a stomachache? (He ate too much junk.)
2. (inferential) What happened to Mother Goat's sewing basket? (Gregory ate it.)
3. (literal) What did Mother and Father Goat do to help Gregory learn to eat junk? (They took him to the doctor and then gave him small bits of junk with his regular meals.)
4. (inferential) Why do you think Mother and Father Goat wanted Gregory to learn to eat junk food? (Mother would not have to make special meals for Gregory, and they wanted Gregory to eat well-balanced goat meals.)

Comprehension Skill Extenders

1. Find out what goats really eat. Compare the foods goats eat to the foods you eat. Which of the foods that a goat really eats might you be able to eat?
2. What do you think is the main idea of this story?
3. Create a recipe for an exciting new goat food you think Gregory would enjoy.

Curriculum Integration

Prepare a one-day menu you feel Gregory and his parents would have enjoyed. Include breakfast, lunch, dinner, and a snack. Then prepare a one-day menu for your family.

CHERRIES AND CHERRY PITS

by Vera B. Williams

Summary

Bidemmi loves to draw pictures and tell stories. She does just that in this book.

Vocabulary

1. subway	3. pocketbook	5. geranium	7. escalator
2. florist	4. bannister	6. stoops	8. beret

Setting Reading Purpose

Bidemmi loves to draw. She tells a story about each of her drawings. Each story has a person who eats cherries and spits out the pits. What does Bidemmi do with her cherry pits?

Questions During Reading

1. (literal) What does Bidemmi like to draw with? (Markers.)
2. (inferential) Why do you think Bidemmi tells each of her stories about cherries and cherry pits? (She likes cherries.)
3. (literal) What does the little lady do with her cherries? (She shares them with her parrot.)
4. (inferential) Why does Bidemmi draw the little brown bag on the lady's pocketbook? (So the reader will be sure that it is there.)

Comprehension Skill Extenders

1. One of Vera Williams' beautiful watercolor illustrations is half of Bidemmi's face. Find a colored picture of a face in a magazine. It should be fairly large. Cut the face out, and then cut it in half. Glue one half on a piece of drawing paper. Sketch and color the missing side, trying to make it look as close to the original picture as possible.
2. In one of Bidemmi's stories, the children's names all begin with "D." Brainstorm a list of as many names as you can that begin with "D."
3. Make a list of other foods you can think of that have pits or seeds. Then survey your classroom to find out which of these foods are their favorites. Create a list that is rank-ordered from favorite to least favorite.

Curriculum Integration

Take a piece of drawing paper. Place a dot on it somewhere. Ask a friend to do the same thing. Exchange papers with your friend. Each of you should then draw a picture on the paper you were given beginning with the dot. After your picture is finished (include as much detail as you can), tell your friend a story about it, and then let your friend tell you a story.

JANUARY

Humor

A PORCUPINE NAMED FLUFFY

by Helen Lester

Summary

Fluffy, the young porcupine, is upset that his name does not seem to suit his "unfluffiness" and decides to change himself. He ultimately discovers that certain things about each of us really should not be changed.

Vocabulary

1. delighted	3. suspicious	5. rhinoceros
2. fierce	4. convinced	6. exhausted

Setting Reading Purpose

Fluffy, the porcupine, is upset because his name is Fluffy and he is not fluffy. Who helps him feel better about accepting this name?

Questions During Reading

1. (literal) Why didn't Fluffy's parents choose the name Needleroozer for him instead of Fluffy? (It was too long.)
2. (inferential) What do you think the rhinoceros meant by, "I'm going to give you a rough time"? (He was going to try and make things difficult for Fluffy.)
3. (literal) Why did Fluffy say, "They should have named me Gooey"? (The whipped cream made him gooey instead of fluffy.)
4. (inferential) Why do you think Fluffy and Hippo became the best of friends? (They had something in common. They both had unusual names.)

Comprehension Skill Extenders

1. Make a list of the most unusual names you have heard. Then make a list of your favorite names. Have a friend do the same thing and exchange lists. See if you and your friend have listed any names that are the same. If you had a chance to choose your own name, what would you choose? Why?
2. If you were in Fluffy's place, how would you have tried to become fluffier? Illustrate your idea.
3. If you renamed Fluffy and Hippo, what names would you choose? Why would you make your choices?

Curriculum Integration

Lynn Munsinger, the illustrator of the story, gave the animals people-like appeal through her drawings. Choose a family of animals normally found in the wild, and draw a family picture of them clothed as they might look on an average day in one of Helen Lester's stories.

THE TEACHER FROM THE BLACK LAGOON

by Mike Thaler

Summary

As a school year is about to begin, a young boy daydreams about who his new teacher might be. A hilarious tale unfolds as he envisions a "teacher from the black lagoon".

Vocabulary

1. dandruff
2. slithers
3. fraction
4. beckons
5. smirks
6. swallows
7. digesting
8. abracadabra
9. headache
10. cackles

Setting Reading Purpose

1. After dreaming about what his new teacher will be like, a young boy awakens to discover Mrs. Green. Describe the "real" Mrs. Green.
2. Why does the boy in the story want to be sent to the principal's office?

Questions During Reading

1. (literal) How does Mrs. Green explain fractions? (She shows a "whole boy," then takes a bite and shows "half a boy.")
2. (inferential) Why do you think the author titles his book *The Teacher from the Black Lagoon*? (Answers will vary.)
3. (literal) What does Mrs. Green do to Freddy Jones after he throws a spitball? (She breathes fire on him.)
4. (inferential) Why did Mrs. Green change the size of Penny Weber's head? (Penny complained that she had a *huge* headache, and a small head couldn't have a *huge* headache.)

Comprehension Skill Extenders

1. Fraction problems are sometimes difficult to solve. If you were a teacher introducing fractions to your class for the first time, how would you explain "one-half" to your class? Create a drawing that you could use as a visual aid.
2. Do some research to find out how a principal spends a typical day. Write a news story about your findings.

3. Write to a former teacher thanking him or her for a memorable first day at school.

Curriculum Integration

Randy Potts was interested in spelling. Mrs. Green's idea of spelling fun, however, was a little unusual.

Design and create a spelling game that you think your class would enjoy. The game could be for an individual, a pair, or a cooperative team. It should be self-correcting.

AN EVENING AT ALFIE'S

by Shirley Hughes

Summary

Rain inside the house? That's just what happens on the night Annie Rose and Alfie are at home with their baby-sitter Maureen while Mom and Dad are out. Everyone plays a part in handling the crisis.

Vocabulary

1. fetch   2. ought   3. brimming   4. mite   5. taps

Setting Reading Purpose

One night when Alfie's parents are out, a water pipe bursts. How does Alfie's baby-sitter Maureen solve the problem of the water leaking onto the floor?

Questions During Reading

1. (literal) Who did Maureen call to help her with the dripping water? (She called her mom and dad.)
2. (inferential) Why did Maureen's mother ask her to bring some towels? (She wanted to mop up the water with them.)
3. (literal) What story did Maureen read to Alfie right before going to bed? (She read *Noah's Ark.*)
4. (inferential) How would you have solved the problem if you had been Maureen? (Answers will vary.)

Comprehension Skill Extenders

1. If Maureen's parents had been home, how would the story have changed? Write your ideas into a new story ending. Draw the final story illustration.
2. If Alfie had fallen asleep quickly and not heard the water dripping, the story would have changed. Write one story change by creating sentences using the following initials to begin each new word (try one, two, or all of the sentences):
   1) M___ W___ N___ H___ H___ T___ D___
   2) T___ W___ W___ T___ C___ T___ T___ C___
   3) T___ U___ W___ B___ F___
3. Brainstorm with a friend and list as many words as you can that have the "sp" sound you find in the story in the word "splash."

Curriculum Integration

It is apparent that a person must be very reliable before he or she can become a good baby-sitter. If you were a parent looking for a baby-sitter for your young children, what kind of person would you look for? Write a description of the ideal baby-sitter from the parent's point of view. On the back of your paper, write a description of the ideal baby-sitter from a child's point of view. How do they compare?

BAD DOG
by Ned Delaney

Summary

When Dog wakes up and finds no food, no water, and no master, he sets off on a search. During his search he continually becomes the bad dog as he lands in one predicament after another.

Vocabulary

1. halt	5. prowled	9. inspected	13. saber-toothed
2. recited	6. timpani	10. Egyptian	tiger
3. escorted	7. soprano	11. mummy	14. brontosaurus
4. conductor	8. ushered	12. curator	15. ornery

Setting Reading Purpose

1. Dog is having a hard time finding his master the Old Man. Where had his master gone?
2. While trying to find his master, Dog is told often that he is a bad dog. What are some of the things Dog does that get him into trouble?

Questions During Reading

1. (literal) How did Dog find his way downtown? (He took the number ninety-nine bus.)
2. (inferential) How did Dog feel when he was at the dog pound? (He may have felt lonely, scared, worried.)
3. (literal) Dog rode in three different types of vehicles. What are they? (Bus, car, and train.)
4. (inferential) Was Dog really a bad dog? Why or why not? (Answers will vary.)

Comprehension Skill Extenders

1. Why is it necessary for cities to have laws saying that pets cannot run loose? What would it be like if everyone in your city let their animals run around wherever they wanted?
2. The illustrations of the city show a large variety of signs ranging from "No Dogs" to "Do Not Touch." List signs you have seen recently. What would the world be like if all signs were destroyed overnight? List some problems that might result. Create a sign that you would like to have in or around your house. Maybe you would like a special sign to be somewhere in your room. Signs have to be very carefully written. Check your spelling before you print the message on your personal sign.
3. If Dog came to your school, what kind of trouble could he cause? What would you do? What do you think your teacher and principal would do?

Curriculum Integration

Do some research to find out the different types of dogs a person can own. If you could own any five dogs you wanted, what kinds would you buy? Explain why you chose each one, and draw a picture of each.

I'LL FIX ANTHONY

by Judith Viorst

Summary

A wonderfully lighthearted story about a younger brother's wishful plotting to get even with his mean older brother when he turns six.

Vocabulary

1. virus   2. clobber

Setting Reading Purpose

Anthony does not treat his little brother kindly all the time. What are some of the ways the younger brother plans to "get even" when he is six?

Questions During Reading

1. (literal) Why will Anthony be tall when he is six? (He will eat carrots, potatoes, and good foods.)
2. (inferential) When he is six, in what ways will Anthony become a better swimmer than his brother? (He'll float, dive, and breathe correctly.)
3. (literal) When Anthony's brother is six, his friends will call him on the phone. Who will call Anthony? (No one.)
4. (inferential) How old do you think Anthony and his brother are in the story? (Answers will vary, but Anthony will be younger than his brother and less than six.)

Comprehension Skill Extenders

1. Create paper bag puppets of Anthony and his brother. Either by yourself or with a friend, act out the story of *I'll Fix Anthony*.
2. The characters of Anthony and his brother have a variety of facial expressions. Take a piece of 12" x 18" drawing paper. Fold it in half and then in half again. You now have four sections to your paper. Draw a picture of your face in each section. Put a different expression on each one, and tell when you might use each expression.
3. Everyone has strengths and weaknesses. One person may be a terrific reader while another may be a super soccer player. Use the reproducible student worksheet (p. 115) to list the members of your family, including yourself. Then list four or five strengths each member of your family has.

Curriculum Integration

In the story *I'll Fix Anthony*, there are apparently two brothers in the family and Mom and Dad. Interview your classmates to find out how many members there are in each family. Then make a graph of your results. You may want to add detail by showing the number of brothers and sisters.

My Family Has Strength!

by_____

FAMILY MEMBER	STRENGTHS

THE BIG SNEEZE

by Ruth Brown

Summary

An amazing chain of events occurs when a fly lands on the nose of a farmer dozing in the barn on a hot afternoon.

Vocabulary

1. dozing
2. alerted
3. scattered
4. panicked
5. fled

Setting Reading Purpose

One day a farmer is sleeping in his barn. A fly lands on his nose. He sneezes. What happens because of his sneeze?

Questions During Reading

1. (literal) What happens to the fly after the farmer sneezes? (It is caught by the spider.)
2. (inferential) Why was the farmer's wife upset? (The barn was such a mess.)
3. (literal) What scared the donkey? (The hens.)
4. (literal) Who woke the dogs and frightened the rats? (The cat.)

Comprehension Skill Extenders

1. The rats fled from the barn. "Fled" is a wonderful word to use in place of "ran." List ten or more words writers can use in place of "ran."
2. What other animal could have been added after the donkey?
   Write two sentences – one that tells about the new animal's reaction to the donkey, and one that tells about what happens next.
3. We can only see the inside of the barn throughout the story. Draw a detailed picture of what you think the outside of the barn looks like.

Curriculum Integration

The story shows the beginning of a food chain (animals that depend on other animals or plants for food). The cat would eat a bird; the bird would eat a spider; the spider would eat a fly; the fly would eat a lettuce leaf.
Draw and label five elements, one for each box in the Food Chain Diagram on the reproducible student worksheet (p. 117). Remember that plants may be part of a food chain. Color each picture when you have finished.

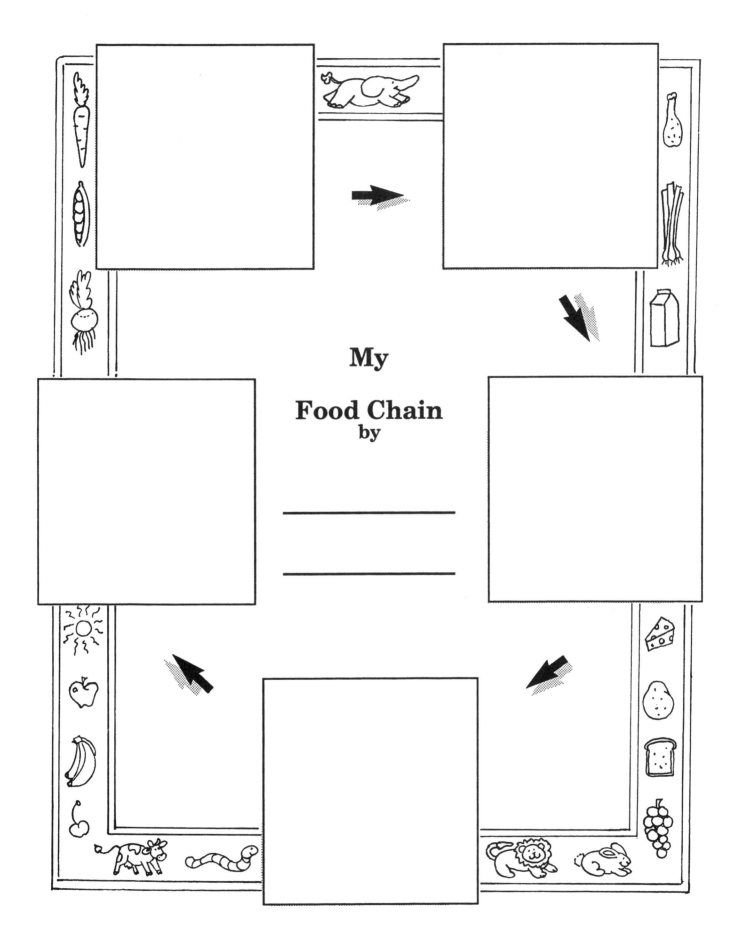

My

Food Chain
by

_____

THE WOLF'S CHICKEN STEW
by Keiko Kasza

Summary

Does the wolf have a soft spot after all? Having spent much time trying to fatten up his chicken stew target, he finds a big surprise when he arrives at Mrs. Chicken's house hoping for a meal.

Vocabulary

   1. craving   2. prey   3. scrumptious   4. screeched

Setting Reading Purpose

1. The wolf is very hungry for chicken stew. How does he plan to fatten up his chicken before turning her into stew?

2. Who lived at Mrs. Chicken's house with her?

Questions During Reading

1. (literal) What did the wolf love to do more than anything? (He loved to eat.)

2. (inferential) Why do you think the wolf did not eat the chicken? (He ended up liking all the chicks.)

3. (literal) What three foods did the wolf give to the chicken in order to fatten her up?
(Pancakes, doughnuts, and cakes.)

4. (inferential) Who did Mrs. Chicken and the chicks first think gave them the food? (Santa Claus!)

Comprehension Skill Extenders

1. The wolf had a craving for chicken stew. If you were asked to make stew for your family for dinner, what would you make? Write out your stew recipe by listing ingredients and giving the procedure you would follow for putting it together.

2. The characters in the story are animals that behave in human ways. Find out some factual information about real wolves in the wild. Write a paragraph of information about the characteristics of real wolves.

3. Why do most people eat chicken meat and not wolf meat? Tell about other more unusual types of meat that people in your class may have heard of others eating or may have tried themselves. Do research to find out some of the more unusual types of meat eaten in other countries.

Curriculum Integration

Animals in the wild eat foods different from what we eat. With a group of friends, put together a recipe book of favorite recipes animal friends might exchange with each other.

For example, do research to find out what types of food an elephant might eat in the jungle. Then create a recipe based on these foods. An elephant might enjoy a recipe of grassland gravy.

Give each recipe a name, and be sure to tell which animal would choose it as a favorite.

Example:

Mr. Bluebird's Rice Pie

1 pkg. wild rice
1 pkg. bird seed
2 pounds of bacon fat
1 pkg. whole cranberries

Mix first three ingredients. Pour in pie pan. Top with cranberries.

HARRIET'S RECITAL

by Nancy Carlson

Summary

Harriet loves ballet, except during recital time. Then she worries about everything from tripping to ripping her costume.

Vocabulary

1. recital
2. terrified
3. audience
4. offstage

Setting Reading Purpose

Harriet is very worried about her dance recital. How does she feel when the recital is over?

Questions During Reading

1. (literal) What is the one part of dancing Harriet does not like? (The recital.)
2. (inferential) What did Harriet do to calm down during her recital? (She took deep breaths.)
3. (literal) What did Harriet think about when she was taking a bath? (Falling.)
4. (inferential) How did Harriet feel after the recital? (She felt the recital was easy.)

Comprehension Skill Extenders

1. Nancy Carlson's dog Dame (a golden retriever) gave her the idea for Harriet. Using a pet of yours or an animal from another story, create a new story character Nancy Carlson could use in her books. Tell about the characteristics of the new character, and draw a picture of it.
2. Create a list of all the characters Nancy Carlson has created for her books. Tell one thing about each character.
3. Write a newspaper article describing Harriet's recital.

Curriculum Integration

Brainstorm a list of ten things a person can do to help get over feeling nervous. Create a cure for nervousness. Make it into a rhyme to share with the class.

IT WASN'T MY FAULT

by Helen Lester

Summary

Murdley Gurdson is often accident prone — until a bird lays an egg on his head. Then it truly is not his fault...or is it?

Vocabulary

1. control   2. valuable   3. confessed   4. aardvark   5. pygmy   6. attached

Setting Reading Purpose

Murdley Gurdson has difficulty with kites in trees, toothpaste control, and dropping valuable vases. Whose fault is it when a bird lays an egg on his head?

Questions During Reading

1. (literal) Who laid the egg on Murdley Gurdson's head? (The bird.)
2. (inferential) Why did each animal say that it was his fault after Murdley began to cry? (They were trying to make him feel better by not feeling it was his fault an egg was laid on his head.)
3. (literal) What was inside the shoe with Eart? (The rabbit.)
4. (creative) How would the story have been different if Murdley Gurdson did not have shoes that were too big? (Answers will vary.)

Comprehension Skill Extenders

1. Rube Goldberg created cartoon-like drawings of inventions based on a chain of events leading to one simple job being completed. Find out more about Rube Goldberg, and tell about one of his unusual inventions.
2. Write about a time when something happened that was unpleasant or silly and may have looked as if it were your fault when it really was not.
3. Murdley Gurdson dropped only valuable vases. Find out about an expensive line of vases by doing some research. How valuable are they? Why do you think they are so expensive? Sketch one.

Curriculum Integration

An unusual chain of events is the reason for the plot development of this story. Create your own story based on four major events. Each event makes another event happen. For example: 1. The rabbit got stuck in the shoe. 2. The shoe frightened the pygmy hippo into accidentally stepping on the aardvark's tail. 3. The aardvark was startled and screamed. 4. The scream frightened the bird into laying an egg on Murdley Gurdson's head.

After you have decided on your four events, create a story by writing your introduction and then retelling each event from the last to the first to explain how something happened. Be sure to write an interesting ending for the story.

WHEN MOTHER GOT THE FLU

by Beverly Keller

Summary

Trying to be quiet and staying out of trouble when Mother has the flu turns out to be far from easy. A young boy's good intentions turn into a humorous adventure.

Vocabulary

1. swatting
2. trampling
3. amazed
4. shimmery
5. scrambled
6. sputtered
7. related
8. tattered
9. slobbering
10. gnome
11. troll
12. entirely
13. demanded
14. shuffled
15. trudged
16. rowdy
17. peculiar
18. disgusting

Setting Reading Purpose

1. The young boy in the story tries to be very quiet and not upset his mother who is sick with the flu. After he accidentally pulls the knob off the television set, gets paint on the rug, and gets melted crayon on the TV, how does he end up in the bottom of a well?
2. How does the boy get out of the well?

Questions During Reading

1. (literal) What is the cat's name? (Lobelia.)
2. (inferential) Why does the cat jump out the window and run away? (She was frightened when the gigantic bubble popped.)
3. (literal) Who helped the boy find his street? (The mailman.)
4. (literal) Why couldn't the boy and the old woman call his mother to tell her he was lost? (They did not have enough money.)

Comprehension Skill Extenders

1. The little boy seemed to think he looked like a troll. Find a book in the library that has a troll as one of its characters. Compare the troll in the library book to the boy in the story.
2. Describe the way you think the little boy would have spent the day if his mother were well. Draw and color a picture to illustrate your explanation.

3. Do you think the little boy in the story chose the best activities to do while his mother was ill? Create two lists. Make one list of activities that are safe, quiet, indoor activities to do at home alone. Make a second list of activities that are better to do with an adult around.

Curriculum Integration

The boy in the story was not always a good problem-solver. What ideas do you have for solving each of the following problems? List as many solutions as you can think of for each problem. Then choose the solution you feel is the best one from each list.

1. The television knob just came off in your hand. What will you do?
2. You just got green and red paint on your cat and your living room carpet. What will you do?
3. You just got bubble gum all over your face and your cat's paws. What will you do?
4. The crayons melted on the top of the TV. What will you do?

123

NO DUCKS IN OUR BATHTUB
by Martha Alexander

Summary

David has a hard time convincing Mom that he should have a pet in their apartment. But how bad can fish eggs be?

Vocabulary

1. apartment
2. pigeons

Setting Reading Purpose

When David's mother won't let him have bugs, pigeons, or ducks in the apartment, he brings home 103 eggs. What kind of eggs do they turn out to be?

Questions During Reading

1. (literal) What does David say about his mother when she won't let him have bugs in the apartment? ("She's a mean old crab.")
2. (inferential) What causes David to realize his mom is pretty nice after all? (She lets him have fish eggs in the apartment.)
3. (literal) Who is David's friend that feeds his fish while he is on vacation? (Mr. Garfunkel.)
4. (creative) What do you think David will do with his frogs? (Answers will vary.)

Comprehension Skill Extenders

1. How could the story have been different if David had been allowed to keep his first pet?
2. Brainstorm a list of ten possible pets. List the good and bad points about owning each one. Then rank-order the list from most desirable to the least desirable pet. (You may wish to work with a friend.)
3. If you were someone's pet, what kind of pet would you choose to be? Why? Draw an illustration of yourself as a pet with your owners.

Curriculum Integration

You are about to open a new business in your town. Your company will provide a pet-sitting service for customers while they are on vacation.

Create a poster to advertise your new business. Be sure to include: the name of your business, the services you will provide, the prices, reasons for choosing your business, a picture that will attract customers, and your name. Your poster should be eye-appealing and persuasive.

THE DAY JIMMY'S BOA
ATE THE WASH

by Trinka Hakes Noble

Summary

When Jimmy's pet boa attends the school field trip, a dull and boring experience turns out to be anything but dull and boring.

Vocabulary

boa constrictor

Setting Reading Purpose

1. When Jimmy's class takes a field trip to the farm, Jimmy takes his boa constrictor along. Although the boa ends up staying on the farm, Jimmy finds himself a new pet. What kind of pet is it?
2. Who tells this story?

Questions During Reading

1. (literal) Why were the pigs eating the students' lunches? (The students threw the pigs' corn at each other, so the pigs had nothing else to eat.)
2. (inferential) What do you think the girl's name is who is telling the story? (Meg.)
3. (literal) Why was the cow crying? (The haystack fell on it.)
4. (inferential) Why was the farmer's wife screaming? (Jimmy's boa was eating the wash.)

Comprehension Skill Extenders

1. When Meg gets home from school, she eats her snack and changes into some rather unusual playclothes. Design some original playclothes you would enjoy changing into after school. What are the unusual features about your clothes? Write a few sentences about them on the back of the picture and be prepared to share your ideas with the class.
2. If you were a farmer, which animals would you choose for your farm? List your choices and tell why you would want each one to be part of your farm.
3. If you were in charge of planning the field trips for each grade level in your school, where would you plan for each grade to go? Tell something about each of your choices.

Curriculum Integration

Do some original research on boa constrictors. Find out where they live, how long they live, what they eat, what are their sizes and types, and other interesting facts. Illustrate your research.

WHY THE CHICKEN CROSSED THE ROAD

by David Macaulay

Summary

At long last, a complex, intriguing answer to the question, "Why did the chicken cross the road?"

Vocabulary

1. stampeded
2. collapse
3. desperate
4. brambles
5. ill-gotten gains
6. investigate
7. promptly
8. picturesque
9. devices
10. substantially
11. stunned
12. reluctantly
13. conducted
14. abominable
15. institute
16. distracted
17. inadvertently
18. assuming
19. hydrangeas

Setting Reading Purpose

1. This story attempts to answer the question, "Why did the chicken cross the road?" What is the reason the chicken crossed the road according to this story?
2. Describe the teacher in the story.

Questions During Reading

1. (literal) What caused Clarella Sweet to fall into Mel Toom's garbage truck? (The explosion caused by the Anderson twins.)
2. (inferential) What kind of animal do you think the bone discovered by Lulu Thump belongs to? Why? (Answers will vary.)
3. (inferential) The police are following a trail of gold coins in search of Desperate Dan. Where does the trail finally end? (It ends at the Clepcoe Mansion.)
4. (inferential) How does this story finally end? (By beginning again with the cows crossing an ancient bridge.)

Comprehension Skill Extenders

1. The story is based on a chain of events that attempt to answer the silly but age-old question about why the chicken crossed the road. Choose another time-honored but ridiculed question and create your own chain of events story. Have at least five linking happenings in your chain. Questions should be unusual ones such as, "Where's the meat?"

2. Create a wanted poster for Desperate Dan that would help police in his capture.
3. Write a short descriptive paragraph about the kind of student you believe Rollo Sweet was in school. Write it from Lulu Thump's point of view.

Curriculum Integration

An important event in history most often is the result of a chain of other events.

A. Choose a war or conflict of historical importance and find out about the chain of events that lead to it. List the events in the order in which they occurred.

B. Interview an adult to find the chain of events that led them to their current job. List those events in the order in which they occurred.

C. Choose a favorite story and list the chain of events that led to the central problem in the story as well as its solution.

THE TROUBLE WITH DAD
by Babette Cole

Summary

Dad's boring job prompts him to spend all his free time in the shed making robots for all occasions. The results are humorous as well as unpredictable.

Vocabulary

1. nagged
2. robotic
3. unbeatable
4. laser
5. operator

Setting Reading Purpose

1. Dad enjoys creating robots that will do many jobs. How does his wife feel about his robot-building hobby?
2. What happens to the robots after they appear on television?

Questions During Reading

1. (literal) What is the trouble with Dad? (His boring job.)
2. (inferential) What was wrong with the slimming robot? (It shrank people instead of slimmed them.)
3. (literal) What did the rich man do with the robots that he bought? (He put them in the Arizona desert and called them art.)
4. (inferential) Why wasn't the robotic hush-a-bye baby improver successful? (Mothers were probably frightened when their babies were thrust so far into the air.)

Comprehension Skill Extenders

1. We can tell immediately by looking at the rich man that he is from another country. What countries could he have come from? Why?
2. If your family was so rich that no one had to work again, how do you imagine you would spend your time? Illustrate your ideas for each member of your family.
3. Dad felt his job was boring. Create a list of jobs you feel would be exciting or interesting and a list of those you feel would be boring.

Curriculum Integration

You have been asked by a large United States company to create a unique new robot that will be helpful to people in some way. Draw a detailed diagram of your robot, and tell how it would be helpful to others.

FEBRUARY

Animals and More Animals

A FISH IN HIS POCKET
by Denys Cazet

Summary

Russell takes in all the sights on his morning walk to school. When he accidentally brings a small orange fish to school in his soggy arithmetic book, he must figure out how to return it to the pond.

Vocabulary

1. shaggy	3. soggy	5. oozed
2. pantry	4. trudged	6. radiator

Setting Reading Purpose

1. Russell loves his walk to school on a crisp November morning. At the small pond an unusual accident takes place. What happens?
2. Russell worries all day about the little orange fish. What does he do with the fish at the end of the day?

Questions During Reading

1. (literal) How does Russell's arithmetic book end up in the pond? (It slips out of his backpack.)
2. (inferential) Why was Russell able to keep time to the music with warm puffs of air? (It was cold outside, and he could see his breath.)
3. (literal) What was the name of the boat Russell made for the little orange fish? ("Take Care.")
4. (inferential) What makes you think the little orange fish was probably not alive at the end of the day? (He did not move when Russell took him from his book, and he kept him in his pocket all day.)

Comprehension Skill Extenders

1. Russell created a little boat out of paper for the orange fish. Using regular writing paper or lightweight drawing paper, see what kind of paper boat you can create by folding the paper. Be sure to give it a name.
2. Do some research to find out a few facts about a type of fish that may be found in another country but cannot be found in or around our country. Sketch it and tell some interesting facts about it.
3. Fish in groups are called schools of fish. Find out what a group of each of the following types of animals is called: geese, cows, wolves, quail, and ants.

Curriculum Integration

Create an aquarium of underwater fish and other aquatic life. Use blue paper for your background. On white construction paper, color and cut out the fish and plant life you would find in a sea or ocean. Add as many details as you can. Cover the entire project with clear wrap. Share your project with your class.

A WEEKEND WITH WENDELL

by Kevin Henkes

Summary

Wendell is having a wonderful time visiting Sophie. Poor Sophie seems to be Wendell's victim until she discovers her own way of turning the tide.

Vocabulary

1. relatives
2. hospital
3. pretended
4. allergic
5. whispered
6. crunch
7. hairdo

Setting Reading Purpose

1. Wendell is an overnight guest at Sophie's house while his parents are out of town. Why does Sophie want him to go home?
2. What does Wendell tell Sophie's parents about eating green things?

Questions During Reading

1. (literal) When Wendell made the rules for playing house, what did Sophie get to pretend to be? (The dog.)
2. (inferential) Why was Sophie always asking, "When is Wendell leaving?" (He was always bothering her and ruining her things.)
3. (literal) When did Sophie's parents say Wendell would be returning to visit? (Never.)
4. (inferential) When do Sophie and Wendell finally become friends? (When they are playing fire fighter.)

Comprehension Skill Extenders

1. Describe a game you would play with Wendell if he came to your house to stay.

2. Wendell wrote his name on the bathroom mirror with toothpaste. Write a message you could read by holding it up to a mirror. You will have to write each letter backward and in reverse order. Then have a friend write a backward message. Exchange and read each other's messages by looking at them in a mirror.

3. Wendell claims to have an allergy to all green foods. List as many foods as you can think of that are green. Compare your list to the one a friend has made.

Curriculum Integration

Have your teacher show you how you can melt old broken crayons together in your clean milk carton by putting the milk carton filled with crayons in the sun. After they are melted into one chunk, use your new chunk crayon to create a picture of something that happened in the story A Weekend with Wendell.

ARTHUR'S TOOTH
by Marc Brown

Summary
Arthur feels bad and miserable because he is the only one in his class who has not lost a tooth. Unknowingly, Francine helps.

Vocabulary
1. complained	3. interest	5. deciduous	7. invented
2. persuaded	4. investment	6. convinced	8. professional

Setting Reading Purpose
1. Children usually begin losing their baby teeth when they are about seven. Arthur, however, has a problem. What is Arthur's problem?
2. Arthur's mother takes him to the dentist to help him solve his tooth problem. What does the dentist do to help him?

Questions During Reading

1. (literal) Who lost her tooth during math class? (Francine.)
2. (inferential) Why did Arthur persuade his father to prepare him steak, corn on the cob, and peanut brittle for dinner? (They were all hard foods to help his tooth fall out!)
3. (literal) What is another word for baby teeth that was used in the movie, "Nasty Mr. Tooth Decay"? (Deciduous.)
4. (inferential) How much money did Francine get for her tooth? (One dollar.) How did Arthur finally lose his tooth? (Francine knocked it out.)

Comprehension Skill Extenders

1. D.W. jokes with Arthur that he will probably have false teeth. In reality, people rarely need false teeth anymore. Do research to find out some of the new methods that dentists have for keeping teeth healthy.
2. Draw a picture of a full set of adult teeth. Label as many teeth as you can with their scientific names.
3. Brain invented a special machine to help remove Arthur's tooth. What would you like to invent to help your dentist? Draw a picture of it. Tell what it is and how it works.

Curriculum Integration

Conduct a survey of your classmates to see how many teeth each one has lost so far. Create a graph of the results using graph paper.

THE FIRE CAT
by Esther Averill

Summary

This is an *I Can Read* book about a cat named Pickles who is always getting into trouble chasing young cats. Then one day her big paws get her a job as the firehouse cat when she truly proves what a big help she can be.

Vocabulary

1. Pickles
2. telephone
3. chief
4. firehouse
5. gently

Setting Reading Purpose

1. Pickles has big paws and truly wishes to do something big because of them. What is the big thing Pickles finally does?
2. What does Pickles do that Mrs. Goodkind does not like?

Questions During Reading

1. (literal) Who was the kind lady who took Pickles into her home? (Mrs. Goodkind.)
2. (inferential) Why didn't the chief ever say anything to Pickles about her work? (He was watching her carefully to see if Pickles could be a fire cat.)
3. (literal) What was the reward the chief gave Pickles when she became the fire cat? (A small fire hat.)
4. (inferential) How do you know Pickles truly learned to like little cats? (She rescued one from a tree.)

Comprehension Skill Extenders

1. Mrs. Goodkind was probably given her name because she is a good and kind lady. Choose people that you know, and give them new names that reflect or tell something about the kind of people they are. Remember that all names must be complimentary. Share your new names with the class.

2. Do firepersons still slide down poles? Call your local fire department to find out. What else can you find out about the job of a fireperson?

3. What is one good fire safety rule? Draw a poster that shows your rule.

Curriculum Integration

Create your own fireperson's hat. Use a 9" x 12" piece of construction paper. Round off the edges. Draw a dotted line in a half circle inside the front of the paper. Cut and fold up. Then decorate your hat with an official fire badge and department name and number.

BEAR SHADOW

by Frank Asch

Summary

Bear is unhappy with his trouble-making shadow. He does all he can to try and get rid of it... without success. The agreement Bear and his shadow make is heartwarming.

Vocabulary

1. cliff
2. pride
3. annoyed
4. cast

Setting Reading Purpose

1. Bear is quite certain he does not like his shadow. What has Bear's shadow done to annoy him?
2. What kind of deal does Bear finally make with his shadow?

Questions During Reading

1. (literal) What scared Bear's big fish away? (His shadow.)
2. (inferential) Why couldn't Bear get rid of his shadow? (When the sun is out, objects block the sun to create a shadow.)
3. (literal) At what time of the day did Bear's shadow disappear? (At noon.)
4. (creative) What is another way Bear could have tried to get rid of his shadow? (Answers will vary.)

Comprehension Skill Extenders

1. What type of bear do you think Bear is? Explain why you made your choice.
2. How are a shadow and a reflection different?
3. Try creating some interesting shadow puppets with your hands. Invent a new one that you have not seen anyone else do. Write the directions for it so someone else could try it, too.

Curriculum Integration

Try creating more than one shadow from the same object. How many distinctly different shadows can you create coming off the same object? (Hint: One light source will create one shadow from each object.)

DUNCAN AND DOLORES

by Barbara Samuels

Summary

Dolores is determined to have a cat even though Faye tries to warn her that animals run away from her. In the end, Dolores learns to change her ways and gain her cat's trust.

Vocabulary

1. disappeared
2. cabinet
3. refused
4. easel

Setting Reading Purpose

1. When a person decides to get a pet, he or she needs to learn how to take care of the pet properly. What does Dolores do that her cat Duncan does not like?
2. How do Dolores and Duncan finally become friends?

Questions During Reading

1. (literal) How old is Duncan? (Four years old.)
2. (inferential) Why does Dolores feel that Duncan likes Faye better than he likes her? (He climbed up on Faye's lap and sat down, and he ran away from Dolores.)
3. (literal) With whom did Dolores have tea? (Her dolls Martha and Mabel.)
4. (inferential) What finally makes Dolores feel Duncan would like to be her friend? (He rolls the paintbrush to Dolores.)

Comprehension Skill Extenders

1. Create two contrasting lists. In the first list, write the names of animals that you feel would make good pets. In the second list, write the names of animals that you feel would not make good pets.
2. If you could have any pet in the world, what would it be? Tell about it and why you would choose it.
3. Create an entry for the "Book of Weird Pets." The pet should be from your imagination. Draw and color it on a piece of 9" x 12" construction paper. Draw it on the top half of the paper. On the bottom half write what kind of pet it is and some facts about it—size, color, favorite foods, anything unusual about it,

etc. Have your teacher add it to the class book.

Curriculum Integration

It is often said that cats have nine lives. Create nine math problems with the number nine in them. Put the nine problems on the front of your paper and the nine answers on the back.

NOTHING STICKS
LIKE A SHADOW

by Ann Tompert

Summary

Rabbit bets Woodchuck that he can get rid of Shadow. But when nightfall comes and it looks as though he might win Woodchuck's hat, Rabbit begins to have second thoughts about losing his friend Shadow.

Vocabulary

1. fandango
2. advice
3. whirlwinds
4. jig
5. exclaimed
6. ushered
7. miserable
8. burrow
9. congratulations
10. wailed

Setting Reading Purpose

1. Woodchuck promises to give Rabbit something if he can get rid of his shadow. What does he promise to give him?
2. What are some of the ways Rabbit tries to get rid of his shadow?

Questions During Reading

1. (literal) How does Beaver suggest Rabbit should get rid of his shadow? (Sweep it away.)
2. (inferential) Why does Rabbit want to get rid of his friendly shadow? (To prove to Woodchuck that it can be done and to win Woodchuck's hat.)
3. (literal) How does Skunk think Rabbit can lose his shadow? (Pull the shadow off Rabbit.)
4. (inferential) When Rabbit's shadow seems finally to be gone, why does he seem so sad? (Rabbit's shadow was his friend. They danced and played together.)

Comprehension Skill Extenders

1. Rabbit tried to outrun his shadow. (Of course, rabbits are quick animals in the wild.) Do research to find out which animals are quicker. List them and their possible speeds.
2. Rabbit loved to dance the fandango and the jig. What are some types of dances performed in our country? Which ones are your favorites? Why?
3. Ann Tompert, the author of Nothing Sticks Like A Shadow, chose to use animals for her characters. How would the story have been different if people had been used? Which do you prefer to read—animal or people stories? Why?

Curriculum Integration

Create your own story using Ann Tompert's key idea:

"Nothing _____ like a _____ .."

Some possible ideas are: nothing pinches like a tight shoe, nothing smells like an onion, nothing cries like a baby, nothing kicks like a mule, and nothing flies like time.

Try to get rid of the tight shoe, onion, baby, mule, or time in your story. You can also make up your own ideas.

GRUMLEY THE GROUCH

by Marjorie Weinman Sharmat

Summary

Grumley is grouchy about absolutely everything until one day when he meets a special grouchy friend. Slowly they discover things that they like, including each other.

Vocabulary

1. gnashed	5. ferociously	9. definitely
2. sloshed	6. horrid	10. first-rate
3. sags	7. unmistakable	11. positively
4. accept	8. artichokes	12. conversation

Setting Reading Purpose

1. Grumley is the neighborhood grouch. Instead of talking about the things he likes, he always talks about the things he does not like. What are some of the things Grumley does not like?
2. Who finally helps Grumley become less grouchy?

Questions During Reading

1. (literal) Why doesn't Grumley like the rain? (It is too wet.)
2. (inferential) Why didn't Nero Pig say anything when Grumley criticized his clock, the draft, and the smell of rotting artichokes? (He was probably hoping Grumley would leave.)
3. (literal) Who does Grumley marry at the end of the story? (Brunhilda.)
4. (inferential) Although Grumley became a much nicer person, he never became fond of rain. Why not? (It kept flooding his house.)

Comprehension Skill Extenders

1. Grumley the Grouch always found at least ten things wrong with his day. List ten things you can find right on a typical day.
2. Grumley the Grouch was not a very good house guest. He complained and hurt others' feelings. Write a "House Guest's Manners Manual" telling exactly how a good house guest should behave. List things a guest should and should not do. Remember that you, too, may be a guest sometime.
3. Grumley and Brunhilda began to list the things they could think of that they liked. Picture frames, dirt, and soft shirts were a few of them. Create your own

list of at least ten of the most unusual things you like.

Curriculum Integration

Grumley the Grouch had some rather comical flooding conditions. As a rule, however, floods can be extremely dangerous. Find out all you can about the famous Johnstown Flood. Tell the class about some of the things you discovered. You can also research another flood.

RABBIT GOES TO NIGHT SCHOOL

by Judy Delton

Summary

Rabbit is bored and is looking for a hobby that suits him. When night school classes in magic are offered, Rabbit finds something that suits him quite by accident.

Vocabulary

1. petunias	6. handkerchief	11. certainly
2. lodge	7. disappear	12. admitted
3. urge	8. amazing	13. agreed
4. improve	9. hoisted	14. excused
5. appealed	10. suited	

Setting Reading Purposes

1. Have you ever felt as if you did not have enough to do and had time on your hands? Rabbit had the time and wanted to find a hobby. What kind of hobby does Rabbit find?
2. Rabbit makes a new friend unexpectedly. Who is Rabbit's new friend?

Questions During Reading

1. (literal) Why didn't Rabbit feel he would like to garden? (The sun gave him a headache, and he didn't want dirt under his pawnails.)
2. (inferential) Why did Rabbit's attitude change from cross to friendly toward Rabbittoo? (He and Rabbittoo began having fun together and became friends.)
3. (literal) What kind of salad did Rabbittoo show Rabbit how to make? (Carrot-top salad.)
4. (inferential) Why does Rabbit say, "I think I know all the magic I need?" (He does not want to lose his new friend Rabbittoo.)

Comprehension Skill Extenders

1. If you were in charge of the local night school in your area, what kinds of night classes would you try to offer? (You want your class offerings to appeal to a large number of people.) List your class titles.
2. If you had a whole day to spend with a friend and could do anything within reason that you wished to do, how would you spend your day, and with whom would you spend it? Create a schedule to show your activities.

3. Rabbit felt that skating was very good exercise. If was also fun. If you could add some new activities to your gym class, what would they be and why would you choose them? Remember they should be good exercise.

Curriculum Integration

Rabbit pulled Rabbittoo from his hat. If you were a magician, what is the most unusual item you could pull from your hat? Create a magician's hat from black construction paper. Draw and color the item you plan to pull from your magic hat. Cut it out.

Attach two paper bands to the back of the magic hat. Slip your creation into the bands. Pull it out as you tell the new story that you have written about Rabbit and his magic hat.

JESSE BEAR, WHAT WILL YOU WEAR?

by Nancy White Carlstrom

Summary

Jesse Bear begins his day by wearing his red shirt and ends up wearing dreams in his head. This is a beautiful story told in rhyme describing a beautiful day.

Vocabulary

1. sprouts   2. moustache

Setting Reading Purpose

1. Jesse Bear is a young bear who has a very busy day. What are some of the unusual things he wears during his busy day?
2. What is the last thing Jesse wears at the end of the day?

Questions During Reading

1. (literal) How does Jesse Bear's name change in the story? (It changes from "Bear" to "Bare.")
2. (inferential) What caused Jesse Bear's moustache of white? (Milk.)
3. (literal) What did Jesse Bear think his pants could do? (Dance.)
4. (inferential) What kind of chair is Jesse Bear stuck in at noon? (A highchair.)

Comprehension Skill Extenders

1. Complete the following rhyme pattern:

   _____ , what will you wear,

   What will you wear in the morning?

   1. My _____

   2. _____

   3. _____ in the morning.

   (Lines 1 and 2 must end in rhyming words.)

2. Jesse Bear wears his "dreams in his head" at night. Describe a dream you have had.
3. What are some things you have "worn" without really meaning to wear? (Example: I tripped in the mud one day and "wore" mud on my hands and knees.)

Curriculum Integration

Jesse Bear takes on the characteristics of a real person for this story. He lives in a house, wears clothes, and sleeps in a bed. What are some of the things a real bear in the wild might wear that are totally different from Jesse Bear? Do some research to find out.

PENROD'S PANTS

by Mary Blount Christian

Summary

Penrod Porcupine has a way of annoying his friend Griswold Bear until Griswold can hardly stand it. Luckily for both friends, a good hibernation promises to help Griswold forget Penrod's irritating ways.

Vocabulary

1. giraffe   2. porcupine   3. invited   4. munched

Setting Reading Purpose

1. Penrod's grandmother Quill sends him a special pair of blue pants. Penrod decides he would like another pair of pants just like them. What is so special about the blue pants?
2. How does Griswold finally lose his tooth?

Questions During Reading

1. (literal) What did Penrod feel was wrong with Griswold's pants? (They were too long.)
2. (inferential) Why isn't it polite to take the last cookie? (Someone else may want it and you would not want to appear greedy.)
3. (literal) What was wrong with Griswold's pants when Penrod was finished repairing them? (They were too short for him.)
4. (inferential) Why was Griswold thankful to be going to bed until spring? (He could try to forget all the problems that Penrod had caused, and maybe he could laugh about them by spring.)

Comprehension Skill Extenders

1. Penrod loved his blue pants for a couple of reasons. Design a pair of pants you think kids your age would want to buy. Add all the details and color, and write an ad to help sell them.
2. Some "good" manners may not make sense to us, such as: "Don't take the last cookie." What is one manner you would like to change? Why would you change it? What would you like to take its place?
3. Think of another way for Griswold to get rid of his loose tooth. Write out the instructions for Griswold to follow.

Curriculum Integration

Like Griswold, bears in the wild spend time hibernating during the colder months. Research to find out what other animals also hibernate. List them. Explain what hibernation is.

MAX, THE BAD-TALKING PARROT
by Patricia Brennan

Summary
Mrs. Goosebump visits Tillie and her parrot Max each day as she returns from work at the tollbooth. Due to an unusual misunderstanding, their friendship is almost ruined. Then Max saves the day.

Vocabulary

1. tollbooth	4. paced	7. bagel	10. hurricane	13. pride
2. tolls	5. tidy-up	8. disgrace	11. sputtered	14. misunderstood
3. wicker	6. astonished	9. crouched	12. halt	

Setting Reading Purpose
1. Max was a parrot with some special talents. While many parrots can talk, Max could also do something else. What else could Max do?
2. What is one of Max's favorite foods?

Questions During Reading
1. (literal) Where does Mrs. Goosebump work? (The tollbooth.)
2. (inferential) Why was Max angry with Mrs. Goosebump? (He thought she said he was ugly.)
3. (literal) How did Max get taken from his home? (A burglar stole him.)
4. (creative) Why do you suppose the burglars stole Max? (Answers will vary.)

Comprehension Skill Extenders
1. Mrs. Goosebump and Tillie liked apple-cinnamon tea. If you were a tea manufacturer, what other flavors of tea would you create? List them.
2. Max realizes after he has said many hurtful things that there has been a terrible misunderstanding because he did not hear a sentence clearly. Get together with four or five of your friends, sit in a circle, and play a game of telephone. Begin by telling something about the story, and see if the last person on the telephone line can repeat the entire original message.
3. When Max was angry and upset, he made up some rather nasty rhymes for Mrs. Goosebump. One of them was: "Keep your hat—it's a disgrace. It might look better over your face." If Mrs. Goosebump could speak in rhyme and wanted to help Max feel less grouchy, what is a two-line rhyme she could say to him?

Curriculum Integration:
Tillie and Mrs. Goosebump enjoyed their apple-cinnamon tea. Survey your classmates about their favorite beverages. Chart the results on the reproducible student worksheet (p. 151).

Favorite Beverage Graph

Surveyor _____

Date _____

Milk	Juice	Water	Cola	Other

Number of selected favorites

Beverage

TWO BAD ANTS
by Chris Van Allsburg

Summary

Two ants in search of crystals for the queen decide to stay in the crystal palace until their adventure becomes far too dangerous. They soon realize, "There's no place like home!"

Vocabulary

1. swiftly	7. anxiously	13. hovered	19. chamber
2. remarkable	8. delicate	14. plunged	20. exhausted
3. crystal	9. ledge	15. violently	21. battered
4. deemed	10. vanished	16. whirlpool	22. amid
5. departed	11. scout	17. bobbed	
6. dusk	12. unnatural	18. shredded	

Setting Reading Purpose

1. Have you ever wondered what things would look like to you if you were very, very small? What are the huge crystals made of that the two ants find so delicious?
2. Why do the ants decide to return to their ant home?

Questions During Reading

1. (literal) Who was the mother of all the ants? (The queen.)
2. (inferential) What was the boiling brown liquid the ants found themselves in? (Coffee.)
3. (inferential) What was the giant silver scoop? (A spoon.)
4. (inferential) Where were the ants when they were shot out like a bullet by some strange force? (An electric wall outlet.)

Comprehension Skill Extenders

1. Put yourself in an ant's place. Of course, everything that seems average in size to us would suddenly seem immense. You have been carried into the refrigerator on a sandwich. Describe your day and how you finally escape.
2. Create a poem that describes a typical day in the life of an ant.
3. Do research to find some true facts about ants. List the five most interesting facts. Then sketch and label an ant.

Curriculum Integration

Examine some sugar crystals under a microscope or with a magnifying glass.

Describe what you see.

Experiment to find out if the temperature of the water matters when dissolving sugar crystals. How long do they take to dissolve at various temperatures from very warm to very cold? Write your hypothesis or guess before you begin your experiments. After your experimenting is complete, describe what you found. Give a definition of a crystal, also.

Example:

Sugar Experiment

Hypothesis:

What I did:

Facts I found:

Definitions I need to know:

153

TYLER TOAD AND THE THUNDER
by Robert L. Crowe

Summary

Tyler Toad simply does not like thunder no matter what the cause may be. Try as they might, his friends cannot convince him to come out of his hole. With a loud clap of thunder, Tyler finds he is not the only one frightened.

Vocabulary

1. disappeared	3. Milky Way	5. waddling	7. gigantic
2. patrolling	4. cannons	6. absolutely	

Setting Reading Purpose

1. We all have probably been frightened by thunder at some time or another. What does Tyler Toad do when the thunder frightens him?
2. Tyler Toad's friends tried to tell him that thunder was harmless. What did they suggest some of the causes of thunder might be?

Questions During Reading

1. (literal) Who was patrolling the forest? (John Bluejay.)
2. (inferential) What did Bluejay, Raccoon, Chipmunk, Badger, and Fieldmouse do when they heard the gigantic clap of thunder? (They jumped into the hole.)
3. (literal) What did Mrs. Raccoon say caused the thunder? (Sky animals were banging on pots and pans.)
4. (inferential) When did the forest animals come out of the hole? (Probably when the sun came back out.)

Comprehension Skill Extenders

1. Many people try to explain the reasons for thunder in nonscientific terms, such as "The Milky Way Patrol is testing cannons." Do some research to find the scientific explanation for thunder.
2. Badger mistook Tyler Toad for a frog. Explain the difference between the two.
3. Create your own imaginary reason for thunder—one that you could share with Tyler Toad. It should be your own original idea, not one you have heard before. Illustrate your idea.

Curriculum Integration

Why are thunder and lightning usually heard and seen at about the same time? Investigate to find out what the connection is between the two.

MARCH

Fables, Tales, and Legends

KING OF THE CATS

by Paul Galdone

Summary

The gravedigger shares an unusual tale with his wife and his cat Old Tom. When his tale is done, the cat mysteriously leaves through the chimney.

Vocabulary

1. gravedigger
2. coffin
3. pall
4. coronet
5. distinctly
6. solemnly
7. shrieked
8. fright

Setting Reading Purpose

The gravedigger falls asleep while he is digging a new grave. What does he see when he wakes up?

Questions During Reading

1. (literal) What question did the gravedigger ask when he got home? (Who's Tom Tildrum?)
2. (inferential) Six cats helped carry the coffin. What were the other three cats doing? (Carrying a wreath and a lantern).
3. (literal) What did the cats do every third step? (They cried, "Meow.")
4. (inferential) Old Tom could do something that a real cat cannot do. What is it? (He could talk.)

Comprehension Skill Extenders

1. This tale was written to be scary. What are the details of the story that make it scary?
2. Tell a friend or a small group in your own words how Tom Tildrum became king of the cats.
3. Black cats are often part of superstitions and scary tales. One superstition says, "Don't let a black cat cross your path." What does this superstition mean? Where do superstitions come from? List other superstitions you have heard or can find in another book. Choose your favorite superstition to illustrate and explain.

Curriculum Integration

In the old tale, Old Tom becomes king of the cats. Create an entirely new folktale in which Old Rover becomes king of the dogs.

DANIEL O'ROURKE

by Gerald McDermott

Summary

When Daniel O'Rourke eats too much and dances too long, he falls asleep under the Pooka Spirit's Tower and dreams a terrible dream. This is an Irish folktale.

Vocabulary

1. mansion	4. misty	8. budge	12. beloved
2. merriment	5. pounce	9. cleaver	13. receded
3. paid his respects	6. reaping-hook	10. decent	14. spout
	7. scoundrel	11. gander	

Setting Reading Purpose

Daniel O'Rourke decides to go to a great party at the mansion on the hill where he eats too much and dances too long. Describe the things that happen to him on his way home from the party.

Questions During Reading

1. (literal) Where does Dan stop on his way home from the party? (The Pooka Spirit's Tower.)
2. (inferential) Was Daniel O'Rourke a wealthy man? Why or why not? (Probably not. He lived in a small cottage with his mother.)
3. (inferential) Why did the eagle leave Dan on the moon? (Dan robbed the eagle's nest.)
4. (inferential) Just before he woke up, how did Dan get so wet? (His mother threw a bucket of water on his head.)

Comprehension Skill Extenders

1. Leprechauns peek out of several pictures in the story. Find out more about leprechauns. Who are they? What kind of magic powers do they have? Then complete the following sentences:

   1. Leprechauns look like _____ .

   2. Leprechauns know how to _____ .

   3. Leprechauns live _____ .

   4. I would like to meet a leprechaun so that _____ .

   5. If I could trade places with a leprechaun, I would_____ .

2. Animal names are often different for the male and female, such as goose and gander. Find the names for the male and female of each of the following animals:
   1. lions
   2. deer
   3. cattle
   4. sheep
   5. chickens

3. Do some research to find out how to do an Irish jig. Share some steps with your class. (Your music and physical education teachers may be able to help you.)

Curriculum Integration

Daniel O'Rourke is an Irish tale. Locate the country of Ireland on a map. The country has been at war within its borders for many years. Why is there a war? Who is fighting the war? How would you suggest that the warring groups try to work out their problems peacefully?

DRUMMER HOFF
Adapted by Barbara Emberley

Summary
A simply told tale of a cannon firing in rhyming verse.

Vocabulary
1. carriage	3. sergeant	5. major
2. corporal	4. rammer	6. general

Setting Reading Purpose
Each person in the army troop has a special job to do to help get the cannon ready to fire. What is the general's job?

Questions During Reading
1. (literal) Who brought the barrel for the cannon? (Corporal Farrell.)
2. (inferential) What kind of physical handicap did Sergeant Chowder have in the story? (He had one peg leg.)
3. (literal) Who fired the cannon? (Drummer Hoff.)
4. (creative) Explain the reason for the last picture in the book. (Answers will vary.)

Comprehension Skill Extenders
1. Draw a sketch of a real cannon. Make it as detailed as you can. How is it different from the cannon in the book?
2. Give a meaning for these words as they are used in the story:
   1. rammer
   2. shot
   3. carriage
   4. powder

   Which of the words are homonyms?
3. This tale is told in rhyme. Cut two rhyming words from a newspaper or magazine and create a rhyme of your own.

   Example:

   My dear grandma gives me   **Money**

   If I say her jokes are   **Funny**

Curriculum Integration:
Look at the "Prime Rhyme Time" cards on the reproducible student worksheet (p. 161). Follow the directions to write Prime Rhyme Time verses.

Prime Rhyme Time

by _____

Choose from each card two words that rhyme and write a verse using those words.

dog	some
wild	can
log	run

_____

_____

_____

_____

thin	fish
Bill	dot
bird	dish

_____

_____

_____

_____

little	say
home	come
find	day

_____

_____

_____

_____

Illustration of your favorite verse

KING GRISLY-BEARD

by Brothers Grimm

Summary

Sendak takes this tale of the 1800s and adds a new twist. A young boy and girl wander into a theater, act out the parts of King Grisly-Beard and the conceited princess, and leave once again.

Vocabulary

1. proud	8. alms	15. scanty	22. fate
2. haughty	9. boon	16. spin	23. grieved
3. conceited	10. avail	17. bargain	24. folly
4. suitors	11. parson	18. wares	25. jeered
5. dukes, earls	12. departed	19. earthenware	26. abashed
6. spiteful	13. wretch	20. pomp	27. bestowed
7. maypole	14. paltry	21. splendor	28. chamberlains

Setting Reading Purpose

The beautiful princess in the story thinks she is too good for everyone who wants to marry her. How does she finally learn to act nicely to others?

Questions During Reading

1. (literal) Why did she call the king Grisly-Beard? (His beard reminded her of an old mop.)
2. (literal) Who did the king vow that his daughter would marry? (The first beggar that came to their door.)
3. (inferential) Why did the princess have such a hard time finding a job she could do? (She had never done any work before because she always had servants.)
4. (inferential) Why did King Grisly-Beard finally tell the princess who he really was? (He felt she had learned her lesson.)

Comprehension Skill Extenders

1. The princess in the story did not say things nicely to other people. When the men that wished to marry her came to ask for her hand, she had something mean to say to each one. One was too fat. One was too short. Others were too tall and too pale. She even made up insulting names for each man. If you were one of her parents, what would you have done?

2. List the advantages and disadvantages of being a prince or princess. Illustrate one advantage and one disadvantage.

3. Do research to find out about the Brothers Grimm, world-renowned tellers of tales. Read another of their tales and retell it to the class or a small group.

Curriculum Integration

The princess tried her hand at weaving and did not have any luck. Give it a try. Take a 9" x 12" piece of black construction paper. Fold it in half. From the fold, cut into the paper to within 1 inch of the edge of the paper. Make these cuts every inch. When all cuts have been made, open the paper. Use 1 inch strips of colored paper to weave in and out of your black paper. Frame if you wish.

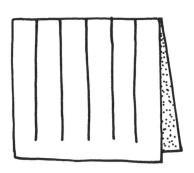

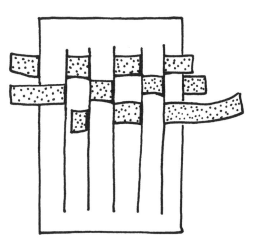

163

THE TALE OF THOMAS MEAD

by Pat Hutchins

Summary

Thomas Mead sees no need to learn to read until a series of events gets him into trouble. With some unusual help he changes his mind about the importance of reading in this lighthearted book of verse.

Vocabulary

1. overhead	4. murmured	7. rammed	10. alphabet
2. disgrace	5. emerald	8. jaywalking	
3. elevator	6. laden	9. cellmates	

Setting Reading Purpose

Thomas Mead stubbornly refuses to learn to read. Why does he finally change his mind?

Questions During Reading

1. (literal) When someone asked Thomas Mead if he could read, what did he always say? ("Why should I?")
2. (inferential) What do you think is the main idea of this story? (It is important to learn to read.)
3. (literal) Who taught Thomas Mead to read? (His cellmates.)
4. (inferential) At the end of the story, how do we know Thomas is happy he has learned to read? (He reads all the time.)

Comprehension Skill Extenders

1. Learning to read is hard for some people and easy for some. What do you think is the most difficult part of learning to read? What is the easiest part?
2. Pretend you are the editor of the school newspaper and you have to write an editorial to convince people of the importance of learning to read. Be sure to write about some things that you can do only if you know how to read.
3. Complete the following sequencing activity:
   Put these events in the order in which they happened by numbering them from 1 to 8.

   ____ Thomas had green paint fall on his head when he could not read the danger sign.

   ____ Thomas went out the wrong door and tipped a cartload of eggs, causing one to land on his head.

____ Thomas pushed the pull sign on the door and knocked down some shoppers.

____ Thomas learned to read when his cellmates helped him.

____ Thomas was sent to jail.

____ Thomas marched into the ladies' bathroom.

____ Thomas jaywalked.

____ Thomas was told that he could not leave jail until he learned to read.

(The correct order is: 1, 4, 2, 8, 6, 3, 5, 7)

Curriculum Integration

Illiteracy is a large problem in America. Many people cannot read well enough to get good jobs. Write a letter to a congressperson telling him or her about your concern and how you think we can begin to solve the problem.

McBROOM TELLS A LIE

by Sid Fleishman

Summary

McBroom's tall tale is filled with colorful whoppers about life on a one-acre farm capable of producing two or three crops a day. Find out how he outsmarts Heck Jones, the would-be farm thief.

Vocabulary

1. kerosene	8. invention	15. trifle
2. genuine	9. ambled	16. slander
3. lugging	10. tinkering	17. scoundrel
4. gracious	11. contraption	18. skulking
5. funnels	12. cylinders	19. mite
6. scamps	13. declared	20. puckered
7. trifling	14. horizon	21. rodents

Setting Reading Purpose

Josh McBroom's children decide to create a machine that will bring them to school so they do not have to walk. When jumping beans do not work as fuel, what do they use?

Questions During Reading

1. (literal) Why did Josh McBroom's hens light up? (They ate so many lightning bugs.)
2. (inferential) How many children were there in the McBroom family? (Eleven.)
3. (literal) What is the one lie McBroom claims to have told? (The cow did not really freeze to death. It just caught a terrible cold.)
4. (inferential) Why did Heck Jones come to the McBroom farm so often? (He was stealing their soil, and he wanted to trade farms.)

Comprehension Skill Extenders

1. If you had to walk five miles to school and could not use any modern transportation, what kind of transportation would you create? Illustrate and describe it.
2. If you could grow crops on McBroom's farm for one week, what types of crops would you grow? Why would you choose to grow them? What would you do with them after they grew?
3. McBroom's story is filled with "whoppers." List five of them and tell how you know they are not true.

Curriculum Integration

Write a tall tale, a "whopper-filled" story, about one of the following topics:

A. One average day at school.
B. One average day at home.
C. One average day with my friends.

MCGOOGAN MOVES THE MIGHTY ROCK

by Dick Gackenbach

Summary

McGoogan, a guitar-playing traveler, befriends a rock that wants to be moved to the sea. A deal is struck to exchange gold for travel help. In the end, however, friendship means more to McGoogan than gold.

Vocabulary

1. blistering
2. weary
3. acquaintance
4. envy
5. confessed
6. bellowed
7. nugget
8. confided
9. reluctantly
10. swift
11. whetstone
12. grindstone
13. millstone
14. milestone
15. burden
16. dunes
17. triumph
18. enchanted

Setting Reading Purpose

1. McGoogan agrees to push an enormous rock to the sea in exchange for the fistful of gold inside the rock. What happens to the huge rock on its way to the sea?
2. What does McGoogan get from the rock at the end of the story?

Questions During Reading

1. (literal) Who asks McGoogan to take the rock to the sea? (The rock does.)
2. (inferential) How does the reader know that the rock is a good and kind rock? (He gives pieces of himself to help people with good projects. He also does not want to be a burden to McGoogan.)
3. (literal) What was one of McGoogan's dreams? (To live in a palace and keep his toes warm.)
4. (inferential) What did the rock mean when it said, "You are a wonder and full of gold yourself"? (McGoogan was a kind and generous friend.)

Comprehension Skill Extenders

1. What are the clues in the story that tell you McGoogan is probably Irish?
2. McGoogan has traveled to many wonderful places. If you could travel to any place in the world, where would you choose to go? Tell why you chose each place.
3. If you could live any place in the world, where would you live? Explain your choice.

4. Use a map or globe to try to figure out how far it would be for you to travel to the nearest ocean or sea.

Curriculum Integration

McGoogan first realized he was nearing the sea when he saw seagulls flying in the distance. It is true that different types of birds are found in different areas of the country. List the birds found in the area where you live. Write a short story about your favorite one.

SIDNEY RELLA AND THE GLASS SNEAKER

by Bernice Myers

Summary

A humorous takeoff on the story of *Cinderella* finds Sidney becoming a football player with the help of his fairy godfather.

Vocabulary

1. motioned
2. stockmarket
3. uniform
4. disappear
5. complained
6. appeared
7. footmen
8. mysterious
9. presented
10. corporation

Setting Reading Purpose

1. (literal) Who helped Sidney Rella clean the house? (His fairy godfather.)
2. (inferential) What kind of uniform did the fairy godfather give Sidney for the tryouts? (A band uniform.)
3. (inferential) How were Sidney's brothers finally convinced he was the mystery football player? (The glass sneaker fit his foot and matched the other one that was presented.)

Comprehension Skill Extenders

1. Compare this story to Cinderella. Make a list of all the similarities.
   Example: Cinderella had to work hard all day. Sidney had to do many chores, too.
2. The fairy godfather was a superhero to Sidney. Create your own imaginary superhero. Tell about his or her magic powers and draw a picture. Tell the name of your superhero.

3. Feet are a very important part of Cinderella and Sidney Rella and the Glass Sneaker. Think of as many words as you can that have the word "foot" in them. List them. Choose one to illustrate.
Example: Foothold

Curriculum Integration

Solve the following problem:

Your mom and dad have to work Monday through Friday until 6 p.m. It is your job to take care of your 3-year-old brother from four until six o'clock every night. Your parents cannot afford to hire a baby-sitter. You are a very good soccer player and have been asked to practice with the winning soccer team every Tuesday and Thursday from 4–6 p.m. What can you do? Brainstorm solutions to the problem. Then choose the best one and tell why you chose it.

THE CAT ON THE DOVREFELL

Illustrated by Tomie de Paola

Summary

An old Norwegian folktale in which mischievous trolls mistake a big white polar bear for a giant white cat. (A Christmas tale.)

Vocabulary

1. Finnmark	4. houseroom	7. yonder	10. fiercer
2. Denmark	5. trolls	8. porridge	11. brose
3. Dovrefell	6. flit	9. lye	12. sideroom

Setting Reading Purpose

Once a man captured a big white bear and set off to give it to the King of Denmark as a gift. On his way to the king's house, he stopped at Halvor's house to rest for the night. How was his rest disturbed?

Questions During Reading

1. (literal) What are some of the foods the trolls liked? (Porridge, fish, and sausage.)
2. (inferential) Why didn't Halvor want the man and his bear to stay at his house? (The trolls scared him away from his home.)
3. (inferential) Why didn't the trolls come back again? (They were afraid of the cat and her seven kittens.)
4. (inferential) Why did the bear chase the trolls out of the house? (The troll put food up against his nose and made the bear angry.)

Comprehension Skill Extenders

1. In one part of the book, two pages that are side-by-side are wordless. If you were writing the story and had to have words on every two-page section, what words would you add?
2. Trolls come in many sizes and shapes. Draw your own original troll. Write a paragraph describing your character.
3. After Halvor told the trolls about the seven kittens, the trolls never returned to his house again. Write a story about where the trolls went for their next Christmas.

Curriculum Integration

You have just received a phone call from a major math book company. They are putting together a new book for which they need some story problems about trolls. Make up a page of four to five story problems. Be sure to illustrate your page. On the back of your paper, write the answers to the problems. Make sure you have problems that require addition and subtraction.

THE DREAM EATER
by Christian Garrison

Summary
Yukio and the members of his village have recurring bad dreams. When Yukio rescues a drowning Baku, the Baku eats the villagers' nightmares allowing them to sleep in peace. The tale is set in Japan.

Vocabulary

1. demon	6. bandits	11. munched
2. devoured	7. brimstone	12. morsel
3. preparing	8. bamboo	13. contented
4. mending	9. honored	14. Mt. Fuji
5. samurai	10. plentiful	

Setting Reading Purpose
1. This Japanese tale tells of Yukio and his villagers who are kept awake every night by bad dreams. How does the Baku help the people of the village?
2. What was Yukio's father's bad dream about?

Questions During Reading
1. (literal) What kind of bad dream did Yukio have? (He was being chased by a three-headed demon upon a dragon with twenty eyes.)
2. (inferential) Why did everyone tell Yukio to go away? (They were all tired and upset by the bad dreams keeping them awake.)
3. (literal) How did Yukio rescue the Baku? (He threw it a vine and pulled it to shore.)
4. (inferential) Why did Yukio tell the hungry Baku he would soon be the fattest Baku in all of Japan? (There were so many bad dreams that he could eat.)

Comprehension Skill Extenders
1. Brainstorm a list of words that could be used to describe different kinds of dreams. After you have created a list of at least fifteen words, choose five of them and draw the dream the words best describe.
2. Do research to find uses for bamboo. If you were given ten long pieces of bamboo, what would you do with them?
3. The older people in Japan are honored and respected as the wisest people in the country. How are older people in the United States treated?

Curriculum Integration

A dream or goal of many people in Japan is to climb Mt. Fuji. Compare Mt. Fuji to a well-known mountain in the United States, such as Pike's Peak or Mt. Rainier. How are they the same and how are they different?

THE FUNNY LITTLE WOMAN
by Arlene Mosel

Summary

The funny little woman who loves to laugh pursues a rolling dumpling. She is captured by the Oni, who puts her to work making rice dumplings until she escapes.

Vocabulary

1. Japan	3. earthen	5. stern
2. dumplings	4. ungrateful	

Setting Reading Purpose

In Japan the funny little woman spends her days making rice dumplings. When a dumpling rolls off the table and she decides to chase it, what happens to her?

Questions During Reading

1. (literal) Why did Jizo Sama tell the funny little woman not to follow her dumpling? (The wicked Oni lived at the end of the road.)
2. (inferential) How did the wicked Oni find the little woman? (He smelled humankind, and the little woman laughed.)
3. (literal) Why did the wicked Oni want to take the funny little woman home? (She could cook for all the Oni.)
4. (creative) How does the illustrator show us that the funny little woman has been away from her home for some time? (The season changes are shown in the sketches of the little woman's house.)

Comprehension Skill Extenders

1. Japanese writing is quite different from American. In the last pictures of the little woman's house, there is a flag with Japanese writing. Do research to see if you can find out what the writing means.
2. The houses in this story look much different from our houses in America. Do research to find a current picture of a Japanese home. How are they different from and the same as ours?
3. Sample a rice cake. What kinds of toppings could you put on a rice cake and have a delicious, nutritious snack? What else would you eat with rice cakes to make a complete meal?

Curriculum Integration

Try creating some original Japanese poetry—haiku. Although we cannot accurately create the pattern of haiku in English, it is best to try to create a mood poem about something found in nature by counting your syllables. Your haiku should have three lines. The first line has five syllables, the second line has seven syllables, and the third line has five.

Example:

Wild geese gliding by.
Free spirits on fleeting wings.
Beautiful fall day.

THE WINTER WREN
by Brock Cole

Summary

When spring does not come to Simon's village, Simon and his sister Meg set out to find it. With the help of the winter wren, Old Man Winter is defeated.

Vocabulary

1. furrows	6. thatch	11. prickled
2. iron	7. meal	12. prune (pruning)
3. daft	8. striding	13. sickle
4. befuddling	9. sowing	14. clatter
5. ravens	10. stalk	

Setting Reading Purpose

Simon and his sister Meg go off to find spring when winter does not seem to end. Where does Simon finally find spring?

Questions During Reading

1. (literal) Why did Simon's mother become angry with him? (They are almost out of food, and he burns the porridge and spills the milk.)
2. (inferential) What do you think really happens to Meg when Winter hits her with a hailstone? (Answers will vary. She becomes the tiny brown winter wren.)
3. (literal) How does Simon think spring looks? (Like a princess dressed in green and gold.)
4. (inferential) How do the villagers and Simon's mother feel when he tells them he woke up Spring at Winter's farm? (They don't believe him.)

Comprehension Skill Extenders

1. Explain the meaning of "daft" by using context clues from the story. List the story clue sentences you used. When you are done, find the word in the dictionary, and compare your meaning to the one given in the dictionary.
2. How do you think the story would have ended if Simon and Meg had not gone to Winter's farm?
3. What is your favorite season of the year? Why? Draw a picture of yourself doing a favorite activity during the season you chose.

Curriculum Integration

The author of The Winter Wren, Brock Cole, did drawings of Princess Spring

and Old Man Winter and told us something about each character.
Draw pictures of characters that you feel show the seasons of fall and summer.
What would you choose to name these characters? Draw them in their favorite
places. On the back of the drawing, write a detailed description of each
character.

ZERALDA'S OGRE
by Tomi Ungerer

Summary

Ogres love to eat children, especially the star of this story. Then he meets a most delicious young lady named Zeralda who truly knows the way to an ogre's stomach.

Vocabulary

1. ogre	6. dumplings	11. capers	16. overwhelmed
2. gruel	7. harnessed	12. concocting	17. menace
3. tepid	8. impatient	13. truffled aspic	18. maiden
4. braise	9. unconscious	14. Pompano	
5. simmer	10. watercress	15. scrumptious	

Setting Reading Purpose

The ogre living outside of the village loves to eat children. One morning he leaves home feeling very hungry, looking for a child to eat. When he sees Zeralda, why doesn't he eat her?

Questions During Reading

1. (literal) When the children were hidden from the ogre, who was out of work? (The teachers.)
2. (inferential) When Zeralda saw the ogre fall onto the road, she decided to help him by making him a meal. Where did she get enough food to fill a giant ogre? (She used her father's market supplies.)
3. (inferential) Why did all the ogres stop eating children? (They loved Zeralda's recipes and used them instead of eating children.)
4. (literal) What job did the ogre give Zeralda's father? (He was in charge of buying the best food in the country.)

Comprehension Skill Extenders

1. Zeralda loved to cook. She started at a very young age to develop her cooking talent. What do you really enjoy doing? How could your talent help you with a job some day?

2. Zeralda wrote all her recipes in big cookbooks she shared with other ogre families. Create an imaginary recipe you think might be right for the ogre and his friends. Give your recipe a name. List the ingredients in it and tell how to mix it together.

3. The village people were afraid of the ogre for a long time. If you lived in the village, how would you get rid of the ogre in a peaceful way without using weapons?

Curriculum Integration

The ogre made up some poems when he felt hungry and grumpy.

Write a song you could sing to the ogre to help him feel happy and calm, and sing it to the tune of your favorite melody.

181

THE GREEDY OLD FAT MAN
by Paul Galdone

Summary

Beware of the greedy old fat man. He eats everything in sight. Luckily a kind and clever squirrel rescues the fat man's victims.

Vocabulary

1. greedy
2. biscuits

Setting Reading Purpose

The greedy old fat man kept getting fatter and fatter because he ate everything in sight. Who finally puts an end to his eating?

Questions During Reading

1. (literal) What did the greedy old fat man have to eat first thing in the morning? (One hundred biscuits and a barrel of milk.)
2. (inferential) How do you know the old man was greedy? (He always wanted more.)
3. (inferential) Which animal could not be caught by the fat man? (The squirrel.)
4. (inferential) Why did the old man follow the squirrel up the tree? (He wanted to eat him.)

Comprehension Skill Extenders

1. Create a new story title by using a synonym for each important word. Write about the character that would be the most important person in this new story.
2. Do research to find answers to the following questions:
    1. How much did the heaviest person on record weigh?
    2. How tall was the tallest person?
    3. How small was the smallest adult?
    4. How big was the largest pair of shoes ever made?
3. Find out all you can about King Midas. How were King Midas and the greedy old fat man alike? How were they different?

Curriculum Integration

Doctors tell us that being too heavy is not healthy. Find out why it is not good to be overweight, and write a short report about how fat affects your body.

If a person is too heavy, how can he or she safely lose weight? You may wish to interview a nurse or doctor.

APRIL

Family and Friends

ALEXANDER, WHO USED TO BE RICH LAST SUNDAY
by Judith Viorst

Summary

Alexander's grandparents give him a dollar when they come to visit on Sunday. Through an unusual, humorous chain of events, he manages to lose it all and ends up with bus tokens.

Vocabulary
1. bus tokens	3. stoop	5. positively	7. walkie-talkie
2. lox	4. absolutely	6. vanished	

Setting Reading Purpose
1. Alexander receives a gift of one dollar from his grandparents and absolutely, positively wants to save it for a walkie-talkie. How does he end up without any money?
2. How did Alexander's brothers feel about his ability to save money?

Questions During Reading
1. (literal) Why did Alexander's grandparents give him money? (He likes money a lot.)
2. (inferential) How much money does Nicholas have? ($2.38.)
3. (literal) How did Alexander try to get his nickel out of the crack that fell when he was walking on his hands? (He used his mom's scissors and a butter knife.)
4. (inferential) How much did Anthony charge Alexander for the candy bar that he ate? (11 cents.)

Comprehension Skill Extenders
1. If your grandparents came for a visit and gave you $5, how would you spend it? How do your choices compare with the choices Alexander made?
2. If your grandparents wanted to bring you an inexpensive but thoughtful gift when they came to visit but they did not like giving money, what would you like them to bring you?
3. What do you think Alexander's best buy was? Why? What was his poorest investment? Why?

Curriculum Integration
Think about something you have always wanted but have not received. Figure out about how much it will cost to buy it either by checking a catalog or ad price, or by calling a store that sells the item.

Decide on some ways you could earn some money to buy it. Make a list of all the possibilities. Then create a personal advertisement poster you could post at the neighborhood grocery or shopping area to advertise your job services.

AMELIA BEDELIA

by Peggy Parish

Summary

The Rogers family just hired a new maid. Little do they suspect that her perception of the English language is so literal that the list of jobs they have left her to do will produce near disaster.

Vocabulary

1. lemon-meringue
2. container
3. fade

Setting Reading Purpose

1. Amelia Bedelia does things just exactly as she is told. When she is asked to dust the furniture, she puts dusting powder all over it. What does she do to the chicken and the steak?
2. Who are the members of the Rogers family?

Questions During Reading

1. (literal) Who does Amelia Bedelia work for? (Mr. and Mrs. Rogers.)
2. (inferential) Why didn't Mr. and Mrs. Rogers fire Amelia Bedelia after all the mistakes that she made? (She made wonderful pie.)
3. (literal) What does Amelia Bedelia do when she is asked to put the lights out? (She hangs them on the clothesline.)
4. (inferential) What did Mrs. Rogers really mean when she said, "Measure two cups of rice"? (Use a measuring cup and put two cups of rice into a bowl.)

Comprehension Skill Extenders

1. There are many words in the English language that have multiple meanings. Think of another instruction for Amelia Bedelia that she might not understand correctly. Write it down and illustrate it.

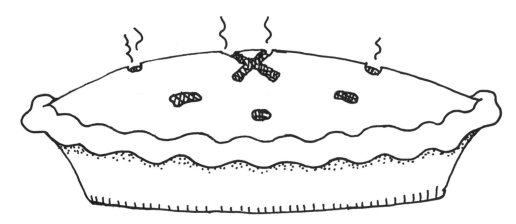

2. The Rogers family loved lemon-meringue pie. Survey your classmates to find out their favorite kind of pie. Give them five kinds to choose from. Make a graph to show your results.

Example:

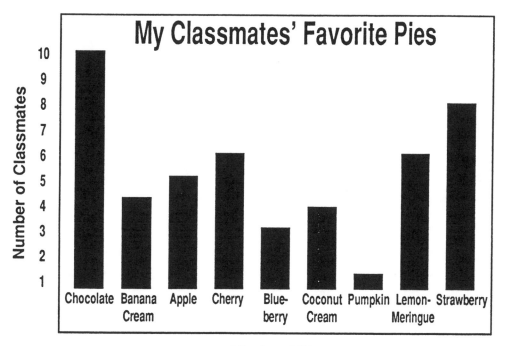

Kinds of Pie

3. If your family had a maid, what would his or her jobs be?

Curriculum Integration

Create a paper bag puppet of Amelia Bedelia, Mr. Rogers, and Mrs. Rogers. Put one character on each side of the paper bag. On the fourth side, write the story title. Then practice telling the story of Amelia Bedelia using your puppet. When you have practiced enough, present your play to a group of friends.

HER MAJESTY, AUNT ESSIE
by Amy Schwartz

Summary

Ruthie is absolutely convinced that her Aunt Essie is royalty. She bets her friend Maisie that she can prove Aunt Essie is a queen by midnight—or she will give her the beloved family dog Joe.

Vocabulary

1. moustache
2. sash
3. proof
4. ladies in waiting
5. butler
6. coronation
7. carriage
8. stoop
9. hustle and bustle
10. magnificent
11. majesty
12. royal blood
13. clucked

Setting Reading Purpose

1. When Ruthie's Aunt Essie comes to live with them, she is sure that she must be a queen. Why does she think this?
2. How do you think Aunt Essie feels about living with Ruthie and her family?

Questions During Reading

1. (literal) What queenly thing does Aunt Essie do when she drinks tea? (She holds her little finger out.)
2. (inferential) Why did Maisie laugh when Ruthie showed her the family tree she drew? (She did not believe Aunt Essie was a queen.)
3. (literal) What did Ruthie see on Aunt Essie's slip? (A crown.)
4. (inferential) What kind of crown do you think Aunt Essie had on her head? (It was a piece of jewelry.)

Comprehension Skill Extenders

1. Ruthie is in awe of her Aunt Essie. Do you have a favorite aunt? If so, explain why she is your favorite. Draw a picture showing you and your aunt doing something you enjoy together.
2. The pictures in the story help describe its setting. In what kind of town do you think Ruthie lives?
3. Imagine what your life would be like as a member of a royal family. Describe a typical day.

Curriculum Integration

Conduct research to find out as much information as possible about Great

Britain's royal family. Prepare a Royal Family Scrapbook. Make your drawings colorful. Include in your book:

A. A family picture with caption showing names of all members.
B. Individual portraits with a bit of personal information under each picture.
C. A picture of the royal palace with information about its location, size, etc.
D. A picture of the royal flag.
E. Pictures of any royal pets.

Example:

Royal Pet

You may add any other pages that may be interesting.

I HAVE A FRIEND
by Keiko Narahashi

Summary

A small boy tells of his very special shadowy friend in simple, poetic form.

Vocabulary

1. whispers
2. underwater
3. warns
4. disappears

Setting Reading Purpose

The young boy in the story has a special friend in his shadow. What does his shadow seem to whisper in his ear?

Questions During Reading

1. (literal) Where does the little boy's shadow live? (In his house.)
2. (inferential) Why does the little boy's shadow keep moving when it is underwater? (The boy is always moving while he is swimming and the water is also moving.)
3. (literal) When the boy's shadow is tall, what can he touch? (The treetops.)
4. (inferential) What does the boy do to try to keep his shadow from moving when it is in the water? (He holds his breath.)

Comprehension Skill Extenders

1. The boy's shadow was sometimes small and sometimes large. When do you think your shadow is the smallest? The biggest?
2. Take a good look at your full-length shadow. Which parts look exactly like you? Which parts look quite different from you?
3. Create a short story that explains "The Reason All Shadows Disappeared From the Earth."

Curriculum Integration

Work in pairs and create silhouettes by tracing around your partner's shadow. Have the student being traced sit in-between a light source and a piece of paper attached to the wall. Trace each other's outline onto separate pieces of paper. When both outlines have been traced, cut out your silhouette and mount it on contrasting paper.

NO FRIENDS

by James Stevenson

Summary

When Mary Ann and Louie move into a new neighborhood, they are convinced they will never make new friends. After Grandpa's story, however, things look brighter.

Vocabulary

1. certainly
2. reflections
3. bounced
4. jackknife

Setting Reading Purpose

Mary Ann and Louie just moved into a new neighborhood. They feel lonely and sad because they have not met any new friends. After Grandpa's story, what happens to cheer them up?

Questions During Reading

1. (literal) What is the name of Grandpa's little brother? (Wainey.)
2. (inferential) How did the Rumbo Gang get its name? (Wally Rumbo was the name of the boy who made up the gang.)
3. (literal) After bouncing through the town, where did Wainey finally land? (In the birdbath on the lawn.)
4. (inferential) What season of the year was it when Grandpa moved into his new neighborhood? (Winter.)

Comprehension Skill Extenders

1. Pretend you have just moved into a new neighborhood and do not have any friends. School will not start for about a month. How will you find some friends to play with till school starts?
2. Grandpa has a way of exaggerating the truth when he tells stories to Mary Ann and Louie. What parts of this story do you feel are probably exaggerated?
3. Compare Mary Ann and Louie's grandpa to your grandpa. How are they alike? How are they different?

Curriculum Integration

It appears there were two children in Grandpa's family – Grandpa and Wainey. There are also two children in Louie's family – Mary Ann and Louie. Survey your class to find out how many children are in each family. Be sure to list brothers and sisters separately. Then answer the following questions:

A. How many children are there altogether in the families in your class?

B. Are there more brothers or sisters?
C. How many children are only children?
D. You may wish to find out the number of children who are the youngest, oldest, or in the middle.

Enrichment:
What is the average number of children in the families in your classroom? (To find the average, add all the numbers of brothers, sisters, and children in the class together and divide by the total number of families.)

NOW ONE FOOT, NOW THE OTHER
by Tomie de Paola

Summary
Bobby and his grandfather Bob are best friends. Bob helps Bobby learn to walk as a baby, and Bobby helps Bob learn to walk after his stroke.

Vocabulary
1. stroke
2. amusement
3. hospital
4. recognize

Setting Reading Purpose
Bobby and Bob were the best of friends as well as grandson and grandfather. How does Bobby help his grandfather after his stroke?

Questions During Reading
1. (literal) What does Bob help young Bobby learn to do when he is just a baby? (He helps him to learn to walk.)
2. (inferential) Why was the last block called the "elephant block"? (It had a picture of an elephant on it.)
3. (literal) When did Bobby know his grandfather would get better? (When the blocks fell down and he moved his fingers and smiled.)
4. (inferential) Why couldn't Bob move or talk when he finally came home? (The stroke made him unable to walk or talk.)

Comprehension Skill Extenders
1. Find out what your first word was and when you said it. Ask your mom or dad to tell you about something silly you did when you were little. Draw a picture of it, and write a paragraph of information about it.
2. Think about the times you have spent with your grandparents. Write about a favorite memory and illustrate it.
3. Our grandparents lived in an era of history quite different from ours. List as many things as you can that were not around fifty or more years ago.
4. Interview your grandparents to find out what changes in our lives they have found to be the most pleasant ones from the time they were young until the present. Ask them to tell you which changes they have not liked very well. Write a brief paragraph of information about your interview.

Curriculum Integration

Oftentimes people retire from their jobs when they are in their sixties. If a man retired from his regular job as an insurance salesman at the age of 65, traveled and pursued hobbies for two years, and then wanted to find a part-time job, what are some possible jobs for which he might be suited?

List as many jobs as you can that could easily be done by grandparents. Prepare another list of jobs that would be difficult for older people to do. Explain why these jobs would be difficult.

LOVE YOU FOREVER
by Robert Munsch

Summary

A young mother finds such comfort in singing to her sleeping son while holding him, she continues the practice throughout her life. When she becomes old and ill, her role with her son is reversed, and a new generation of song-singing begins.

Vocabulary

1. teenager
2. daughter

Setting Reading Purpose

1. All through her son's life, the mother sings him this song: "I'll love you forever, I'll like you for always, As long as I'm living my baby you'll be." What does the son do for his own child when he grows up?
2. What did the son do for his mother when she became old and sick?

Questions During Reading

1. (literal) When the baby was two, what did he do with his mother's watch? (He flushed it down the toilet.)
2. (inferential) What kind of pet did the boy have throughout his life? (A cat.)

3. (literal) Where did the boy move when he was grown up? (He moved to his own home across town.)
4. (creative) Why did the mother sing to her son when he was asleep? (Answers will vary.)

Comprehension Skill Extenders

1. The central theme of the story revolves around a song the mother sings to her son. Create a song of your own you would like to sing to your children someday or that you would like your parents to sing to you.
2. The story tells how the baby boy went through changes in his personality as he grew up. What are some changes you have gone through?
3. People go through various stages of life: baby, child, teenager, young adult, adult, old person. Which stage do you think will be the most difficult? The easiest? Why?

Curriculum Integration

Families are important to most everyone. Create a portrait of your family using watercolor paints. Tell something special about each member.

CALEB AND KATE

by William Steig

Summary

Caleb and Kate love each other dearly. After a silly argument, Caleb is transformed into a dog. Only then do Caleb and Kate realize how important each one is to the other.

Vocabulary

1. odious
2. pondering
3. cantankerous
4. wheezed
5. slavered
6. brogans
7. stunned
8. dread
9. deserted
10. woebegone
11. catastrophe
12. reluctant
13. gravely
14. traipsed
15. glimpse
16. bereft
17. cronies
18. reveling
19. transformation
20. roving
21. extraordinary
22. catapulted
23. deftly
24. pummeled
25. fend
26. intruders
27. astounded
28. exultantly
29. cleaved
30. breeches

Setting Reading Purpose

After Caleb and Kate have a silly fight, Caleb is turned into a dog by a passing witch. How does he become Caleb again?

Questions During Reading

1. (literal) Who taught the witch the spell she used on Caleb? (Her cousin Iggdrazil.)
2. (inferential) What frightened the thieves? (Seeing a dog that changed into a man.)
3. (literal) Who was responsible for injuring Rufus? (The tallest burglar.)
4. (creative) What did Caleb mean when he thought he did not want to forget who he was? (Answers will vary.)

Comprehension Skill Extenders

1. We sometimes come across words we do not know the meaning of while reading a new story. It is often possible to figure out the meaning by working to understand the sentence the word is in as well as the sentences around it. This is called using context clues. Use context clues to help you determine the meanings for the following words: pondering, breeches, dread, reluctant, and traipsed. Then use a dictionary to see how well you did.

2. Steig uses powerful word choices. List as many words as you can find in the story that take the place of "said."

3. Rufus the dog could learn tricks quickly which amazed Kate. If you had a very intelligent pet dog and wanted to teach it one amazing or unusual trick, what would you teach it to do?

Curriculum Integration

Yedida could have easily changed Caleb into something other than a dog. Rewrite the story with Yedida changing Caleb into the animal of your choice. How will this new character get along with Kate, and how will it turn back into Caleb again?

MY MOTHER NEVER LISTENS TO ME

by Marjorie Weinman Sharmat

Summary

Jerome is unhappy that his mother always seems to be busy reading a book or doing something else when she should be listening to him. He tries creating wild and unusual stories to get his mother's attention.

Vocabulary

1. commanded	3. marvelous	5. prickles	7. Jerome
2. detergent	4. bandit	6. slouch	8. Penelope

Setting Reading Purpose

1. Jerome's mom is so busy reading her book that she does not have time to listen to him. How does he finally get her attention?
2. How do you know Jerome is a child with a good imagination?

Questions During Reading

1. (literal) To get his mom's attention, what does Jerome say he wants to be when he grows up? (A bandit.)
2. (inferential) Why do you think Jerome is trying so hard to get his mother to pay attention to him? (Possible answer: He wants someone to talk to and do something with him.)
3. (literal) Why does Jerome have little prickles on his neck? (He tells his mother there is a giant leaning over his shoulder and it scares him.)
4. (inferential) Why do you think Jerome's mother does not like Penelope? (Answers will vary.)

Comprehension Skill Extenders

1. Jerome's mom seems not to be paying attention. What are some things you would do to gain attention if your parents seemed too busy to listen?
2. Jerome's mom does not seem to want him to play with Penelope. Should parents have the right to tell their children they may not play with certain kids? Why or why not? (If possible, interview an older child about this question. How does your answer compare to his or hers?)
3. Jerome has a wonderful imagination. He creates a scary giant in his mind that will scare his mother. Draw or paint your best imaginary giant. How would you describe it to your mom or dad if you wanted to get his or her attention? Write your description on the back of the drawing.

Curriculum Integration

Create a "flip book" about things your mom (or another adult you know) loves and things she hates. You will need six to eight blank index cards. Punch holes in the tops of the cards and attach them with yarn to make a book. The outside cards are the covers, front and back:

On the fronts of all six to eight cards, write about what your mom loves, as in the following example:

Flip the card book over and write on the backs of all the cards some things your mom hates, as in the following example:

Use thumbprints or small drawings to illustrate your ideas. You may wish to include a page about the author.

TELL ME A MITZI
by Lore Segal

Summary

Three humorous stories about life as a child in a gentle, large city.

Vocabulary

1. elevator
2. doorman   Mitzi Takes a Taxi
3. exhausted

1. terrible
2. temperature   Mitzi Sneezes
3. thermometer

1. trouser
2. motorcyclist
3. president   Mitzi and the President
4. Secret Service
5. fantastic

Setting Reading Purpose

1. Mitzi has a way of making every day sound like an adventure. What happens when Jacob yells for the president's parade to come back?
2. Who took care of Mitzi's mother when she got sick?

Questions During Reading

1. (literal) After Jacob and Mitzi got into the taxi, why couldn't they go to Grandma and Grandpa's house? (They didn't know the address.)
2. (inferential) What is a "Mitzi"? (It is both a story and the name of a little girl.)
3. (literal) Why was the chewing gum shop closed? (The workers went to the parade.)
4. (inferential) Why did Mitzi's family tell her mother that she could not go to bed? (They needed her to take care of them.)

Comprehension Skill Extenders

1. Mitzi, Jacob, and her father saw a presidential parade. Describe a parade you would most like to see. What things or people would parade by you? Where would the parade take place?
2. Make up your own "Mitzi" about something that has really happened to you and your family.

3. Having a cold is not any fun at any time. Scientists have no cure for a cold. Do research to find out the reason people get colds. What is the best thing to do to get rid of a cold?

Curriculum Integration

Read Lore Segal's book entitled *Tell Me A Trudy*. Compare the two books. How are they the same and different? Explain which book is your favorite and why.

THE PERFECT FAMILY
by Nancy Carlson

Summary

Louanne Pig is an only child who thinks her friend George is lucky to have five sisters and four brothers. After staying with George's family for the weekend, she better appreciates her own small family.

Vocabulary

1. dull   2. perfect   3. adopting   4. ignore   5. discovery

Setting Reading Purpose

1. Louanne Pig longs to be part of a big family. How many children are there in her family?
2. How does Louanne feel about large families after staying at George's house?

Questions During Reading

1. (literal) Why did Louanne spend the weekend at George's house? (Her parents were out of town.)
2. (inferential) How many people were there in George's family? (Twelve: ten kids and two parents.)
3. (literal) How did Louanne fall down? (She tripped on Hal's rollerskate and fell.)
4. (creative) What does it mean when someone says, "Just ignore him and he'll go away"? (Usually if you do not notice a person and his activity, he will stop trying to get your attention.)

Comprehension Skill Extenders

1. Louanne Pig misses several things about her home such as the quiet and her mom's potato salad. If you were gone for several days, what would you miss the most about your home and why?
2. George's house does not always seem to be very organized—Hal leaves his toys lying around; Nancy gets into Louanne's suitcase.
   A. What kinds of rules do you have at your home that help keep it running smoothly?
   B. What is one rule you would like to make around your home if you could make any rules? Why would you make that choice?
3. The cover of the book has a family portrait of Louanne Pig's family. Draw a family portrait of your family. Make it as detailed as possible.

Curriculum Integration

In this story, rabbits and pigs live happily together. Do research to find out how rabbits and pigs are alike and how they are different. Use the reproducible student worksheet (p. 205) to record your information.

Research Comparisons

by _____

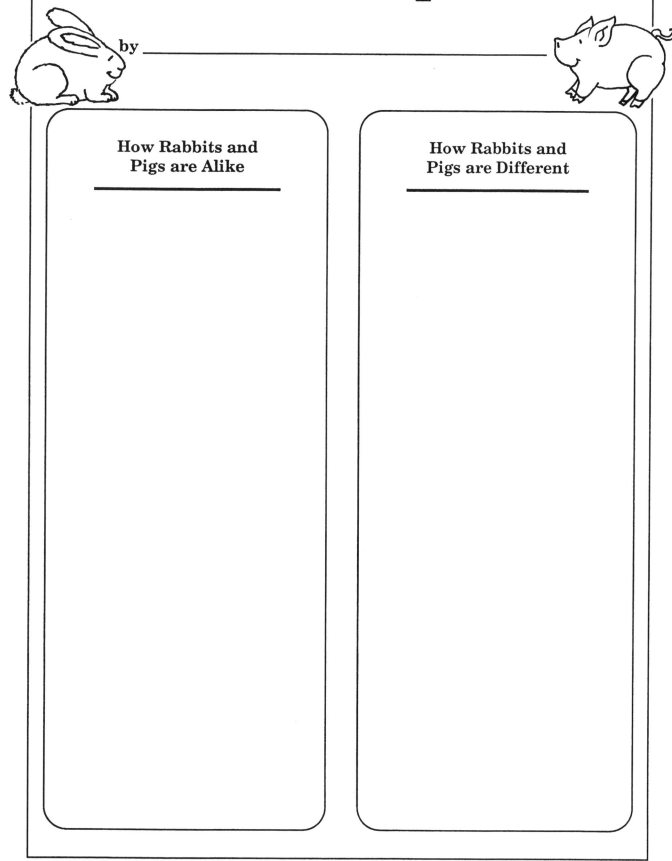

How Rabbits and Pigs are Alike	How Rabbits and Pigs are Different

APRIL FOOL
by Mary Blount Christian

Summary

Seth the Dreamer comes up with a foolish yet ingenious plan to prevent the king and his men from seizing the road through his town. Legend has it that he may have also started the first April Fool's Day.

Vocabulary

1. candlemaker	4. blacksmith	7. plough	10. whey
2. tax collector	5. tantrum	8. clever	
3. game warden	6. moaned	9. brayed	

Setting Reading Purpose

1. King John is about to visit the city of Gotham to see if he would like to build a house there and come to visit and hunt and travel. How do the people of Gotham feel about having a king for a neighbor?
2. Why does the King decide that he does not want to visit Gotham?

Questions During Reading

1. (literal) What did the grownups of the village call Seth? (Seth the Dreamer.)
2. (inferential) Why didn't the people of the village want King John to build a house in their village? (It would become noisy, unsafe, and too much work for the villagers.)
3. (literal) When did King John ride into Gotham? (April 1st.)
4. (inferential) How did Seth save the town? (He dreamed up a plan to make the king feel that the town was filled with fools who would be of no help to him.)

Comprehension Skill Extenders

1. The town in the story had jobs for candlemakers, bakers, tax collectors, blacksmiths, and farmers. What kinds of jobs do you find people do in your town today? What kinds of jobs do your friends and family members do?
2. The townspeople kept reminding Seth of all the things dreams cannot do. What are some of the things dreams can do? Why do you think people daydream?
3. Find some factual information about King John of England and his family. He was a real king during the thirteenth century. What kind of king was he? What is he remembered for? Of which famous present-day family is he an ancestor?

Curriculum Integration

Prince Charles of England is scheduled to visit your town next week. Your family is responsible for making his three-day stay a pleasant one. Complete the reproducible student worksheet (p. 207) to plan for his visit.

Friendly Royal Visit

Planning Worksheet

Prepared by _____

Place where the Prince will stay: _____

Restaurants that will serve him: _____

_____

_____

Friends to be introduced to His Majesty:

_____

_____

Entertainment possibilities:

_____

_____

He is expecting to visit in our home.

He will meet_____

_____

Our special family meal to be served is _____

_____

I will show him my _____

_____

We will talk about _____

_____

THE TERRIBLE THING THAT HAPPENED AT OUR HOUSE

by Marge Blaine

Summary

A sensitive, appealing look at the changes that occur in a family when Mom goes back to work as a science teacher.

Vocabulary

1. afterward
2. terrible
3. important
4. frankfurters
5. annoying
6. spark plugs
7. salmon croquettes
8. laundry
9. bothering
10. decided
11. allergy

Setting Reading Purpose

1. If your mom has always been at home, it takes some adjusting when she goes to work. How do the kids in the story help out at home when their mom goes back to work?
2. How did the little girl in the story feel about having her mother go back to work?

Questions During Reading

1. (literal) What was *The Terrible Thing That Happened At Our House*? (Mom went back to work as a science teacher.)
2. (inferential) What did Mom mean in the story when she said that she needed time "to clear her head"? (She needed to relax for awhile.)
3. (literal) Why didn't the little girl like reading stories to her brother? (She thought he chose "boring books and asked dumb questions.")
4. (inferential) Why did the little girl get so mad when no one passed her more milk? (She really was angry about all the changes in the family's routine when her mother went back to work.)

Comprehension Skill Extenders

1. The children in the story did not seem to have many chores to do around home until their mom went back to teaching. What kinds of jobs do you have to do around your home? How do you feel about doing them?
2. The story did not mention the children receiving an allowance. How do you feel about children getting an allowance? What should they have to do to earn one, and how much money is fair?

3. How valuable do you think this book is as a resource for kids? Would you recommend that libraries buy this book? Why or why not?

Curriculum Integration

One of the illustrations in the book shows a suggestion box. This is often a good way for busy groups of people to sit down and talk about problems. Use an empty shoe box to create a suggestion box for your home. Cover the box with paper. Decorate it. Put the words "Suggestion Box" on the side.

Then design a family letter informing your family of ways to use the suggestion box. Set up guidelines for the kinds of ideas that can be put into the suggestion box, who will read the suggestions, and how they can be discussed. Think of and put into practice other ways to use the suggestion box as an aid in family communication.

MR. WINK AND HIS SHADOW, NED
by Dick Gackenbach

Summary

Ned and his shadow are wonderful companions until they get into a silly quarrel and discover the sadness that comes with losing a friend.

Vocabulary

1. tiff
2. wits
3. gloomy
4. oath
5. ward
6. flickering
7. rascal
8. fierce
9. awning
10. downhearted
11. ill-tempered

Setting Reading Purpose

1. Mr. Wink and his shadow Ned have wonderful times together until they separate because of a silly argument. What is their argument about?
2. What was Ned's secret?

Questions During Reading

1. (literal) How does Ned scare the wits out of Mr. Wink? (Ned would jump up behind him.)
2. (inferential) Why was Mr. Wink so upset about not knowing where Ned went on rainy days? (He thought Ned felt he was not good enough to share secrets with him.)
3. (literal) How did Ned get to Florida? (He rode in the shadow of a balloon.)
4. (creative) Would you have shared your secret with Mr. Wink if you were in Ned's place? (Answers will vary.)

Comprehension Skill Extenders

1. Mr. Wink would never know the secret of where Ned went on rainy days. Do some research on shadows to see if you can find the answer to the secret.
2. Describe times when you can and cannot control your shadow.
3. If you wanted to have your shadow around as much as possible, where would be the best places in the world to live? Why?

Curriculum Integration

Make an outline of Mr. Wink and Ned on a piece of cardboard. Cut them out and attach them to tongue depressors. Create a puppet stage with a light source (such as a projector light) behind it.

Practice telling the story of Mr. Wink and Ned, and then give a shadow play for your friends.

MAY

Sports and Award Winners

SUPER BOWL

by Leonard Kessler

Summary

The Animal Champs and the Super Birds meet for the big Super Bowl Game. This is a simple explanation of Super Bowl championship play for the beginning reader.

Vocabulary

1. kickoff
2. referee
3. huddle
4. end zone
5. sideline

Setting Reading Purpose

The Animal Champs and the Super Birds are playing in the Super Bowl Game. Who becomes the hero of the game?

Questions During Reading

1. (literal) Who was the referee of the game? (Fox.)
2. (inferential) Why did Goose kick Turtle? (She was angry because Turtle hit her.)
3. (literal) Who won the Super Bowl Game? (Animal Champs.)
4. (inferential) Just before the two-minute warning, Duck dropped the ball. Why did he drop it? (Duck tripped on the water bucket which fell on his head and caused him to drop the ball.)

Comprehension Skill Extenders

1. Some animals have special strengths that might be of great value to real football players. Name animals that have special characteristics that would be good for football players. Tell what those talents are for each animal.
2. List as many teams as you can that have won the Super Bowl.
3. Players who win a Super Bowl game receive a coveted Super Bowl ring. Sketch the top view of a Super Bowl Ring for the next Super Bowl. Then sketch a side view. Explain the meaning of your design.

Curriculum Integration

Do some research to find out how football was first invented.

MISS NELSON HAS A FIELD DAY

by Harry Allard and James Marshall

Summary

Smedley School is beset by gloom as the Smedley Tornadoes football team fails to score one single point all season. Viola Swamp comes to the rescue with surprising results.

Vocabulary

1. gloom	4. mincemeat	7. rummaging	10. probably
2. depressed	5. discussion	8. tackle	
3. pitiful	6. substitute	9. disturb	

Setting Reading Purpose

When the Smedley School football team, the Tornadoes, cannot even score one point, the entire school becomes very sad and gloomy. Why does the football team finally shape up?

Questions During Reading

1. (literal) What did Mr. Blandsworth do when he got depressed about the football team not winning any football games? (He hid under his desk.)
2. (inferential) Who did Miss Nelson call after she found her ugly black sweatsuit? (She called her sister Barbara.)
3. (literal) What was the score of the big Thanksgiving Day Game? (Tornadoes 77 - Werewolves 3.)
4. (inferential) Who was Viola Swamp? (Miss Nelson.)

Comprehension Skills Extenders

1. Viola Swamp has a sweatshirt that says, "Coach and Don't You Forget It." Design a sweatshirt you think football players or coaches might buy. Remember, it should have a catchy slogan.
2. Name the football team from each of the following places:
   1. Minnesota
   2. Green Bay, Wisconsin
   3. Los Angeles, California
   4. New York
   5. Chicago
   6. Denver

3. Do some research to find out which football team has played the most Super Bowl games.

Curriculum Integration

Compare the skills needed to play football to those needed to play baseball. How are they the same and different?

Why do you think we do not have any professional women's football leagues?

HOORAY FOR SNAIL

by John Stadler

Summary

An improbable easy-to-read story of a very slow and tired snail who has the determination to somehow make a home run.

Vocabulary

1. thirsty   2. fielder

Setting Reading Purpose

Snail is small and very slow. After he hits the baseball, what does he do?

Questions During Reading

1. (inferential) What does Snail do right after he hits the ball? (He tips his hat.)
2. (inferential) Which animal is the manager of the baseball team? (The hippo.)
3. (literal) What does the fielder do with the ball when it comes down? (He throws the ball.)
4. (inferential) Why was Snail safe? (The catcher dropped the ball.)

Comprehension Skill Extenders

1. Make up a two-line rhyme about a sport that you like.
   Examples:

   > Kicking a football far
   > Makes me feel like a star.

   > With my bat and my ball
   > I feel very tall.

   > Learning to skate
   > Can make you feel great.

2. Do some research to find answers to these questions:
   A. Where do snails live?
   B. What do snails eat?
   C. What animals eat snails?
   D. Would a snail make a good pet? Why or why not?
3. If you had to make up a baseball team of nine different animals, which animals would you choose? Why would you choose each one?
   Example: I would choose the cheetah for speed.

Curriculum Integration

Unscramble the letters on the reproducible student worksheet (p. 217) to find animal names.

Animal Confusion

Name _____

Unscramble the following animal words and draw a line from each to its matching picture.

1. i g p _____

2. g r o f _____

3. s o g o e _____

4. l n i s a _____

5. e r b a _____

6. i p h o p _____

7. n o l i _____

8. t g r i e _____

9. g d o _____

10. o o e m s _____

Write about or illustrate one of these animals as it ice skates.

MAKING THE TEAM
by Nancy Carlson

Summary

Louanne practices for cheerleading tryouts. Her friend Arnie wants to try out for the football team. The results of their efforts are both surprising and delightful.

Vocabulary

1. exciting	6. cartwheels	11. rarely
2. bulletin board	7. ought	12. encouraged
3. cheerleading	8. tackling	13. confidence
4. squad	9. tryouts	14. consoled
5. practice	10. improve	

Setting Reading Purpose

Louanne wants to try out to become a cheerleader while her friend Arnie wants to become a member of the football team. What activities do Louanne and Arnie finally become involved in?

Questions During Reading

1. (literal) What happened when Louanne first threw the football to Arnie? (He missed it.)
2. (inferential) How did Arnie make Louanne feel better when she was not chosen to become a cheerleader? (He told her she would be much better next year.)
3. (literal) Who asked Louanne to try out for the football team? (Coach Ed.)
4. (inferential) What was the name of the football team at Arnie and Louanne's school? (The Bulldogs.)

Comprehension Skill Extenders

1. Cheerleaders have a series of rhymes or chants about their school that they yell out as they cheer. Create a school cheerleading chant your class could use if they played football against a class from another school.
   Example: Strawberry shortcake
          Blueberry Pie
          V-I-C-T-O-R-Y
          Go, Bulldogs!
2. Nancy Carlson dedicated this book to the memory of her dog Dame. Write a short story telling about your favorite pet. If you have never had a pet, tell about a pet you would like to have.

3. Think of as many words as you can that rhyme with each of the following words:

    A. Football
    B. Tryout
    C. Team
    D. Jump
    E. Kick
    F. Fall

Curriculum Integration

Louanne and Arnie were truly good friends. They encouraged and helped each other. Friendship is important to everyone. Write a letter to Louanne and Arnie telling them why you think you are a good friend to others.

MAX

by Rachel Isadora

Summary

Max loves to play baseball with his friends. He develops surprising new Saturday baseball warmups when he goes to dance class with his sister.

Vocabulary

1. sneakers
2. barre
3. pas de chat

Setting Reading Purpose

Max loves baseball and plays it every Saturday with his team. Every good baseball player needs to warm up before a game. How does Max warm up?

Questions During Reading

1. (literal) Where do Max and his team play baseball? (In the park.)
2. (inferential) Why does Max go into Lisa's dance class? (He has time before his game, so he goes inside to wait.)
3. (literal) What does Max do at the barre? (He stretches.)
4. (creative) Why do you think Max likes to go to Lisa's dance class? (Answers will vary.)

Comprehension Skill Extenders

1. People can take many different types of dance lessons. Lisa and her dance class were learning ballet. If you took dance classes, what kind of dancing would you want to learn? Why?

2. Baseball players wear uniforms to represent different teams. Design a baseball uniform for the members of your class to wear if you were all members of the same baseball team. Create a colored picture of all the parts of your uniform. What would you name your team?

3. You have just arrived in a new town as the manager of the community sports association. You need to organize teams of adults and children to play in different sporting events. Create a newspaper ad to advertise and promote your favorite sport. Tell why it would be fun to get involved on a team; who can sign up; and when, where, and how long the season will last. Are there any costs involved? Add appealing artwork to your ad.

Curriculum Integration

From nonfiction books about the sport of baseball, find an important and interesting fact to write down and illustrate. Encourage each member of your class to do the same thing. Put them together to create your own class book of baseball trivia or baseball facts.

TWO STRIKES FOUR EYES
by Ned Delaney

Summary

Toby, the mouse, loved everything about baseball, but he was terribly nearsighted and afraid to wear his glasses until it was almost too late.

Vocabulary

1. whiskers	5. pegged	9. outstanding	13. appreciation
2. athletes	6. dreaded	10. dugout	
3. spectacular	7. physical	11. resounding	
4. grounders	8. championship	12. astonished	

Setting Reading Purpose

Toby is afraid to wear his glasses in front of his baseball team. He does not want to be called names like Sissy or Four Eyes. What does his team do when they finally see him in his glasses?

Questions During Reading

1. (literal) Why did Toby get on the team when he was playing so badly? (They needed someone to take the place of Oscar Peppercorn.)
2. (inferential) Why did Toby play baseball so badly? (He could not see the ball without his glasses.)
3. (literal) Which two teams played in the championship game? (Rodents and Fowls.)
4. (inferential) Who was the pitcher for the Fowls in the championship game? (Rhode Island Red.)

Comprehension Skill Extenders

1. Answer this question: Would you rather be a baseball or a bat? Why did you make your choice?
2. When we think about baseball, we may have some of the following words come to mind: spring, ball, bat, glove, uniform, running, fun, hotdogs, spikes. List as many words as you can for each of the following: football, friendship, cleaning, home, glasses.
3. Pretend that Toby became a world-famous baseball player. Create a baseball card that you might add to your baseball collection. On the front would be his picture (Toby's picture). The back would have baseball statistics like hits; runs batted in; batting average; and personal information like age, height, weight, college attended.

Curriculum Integration

Two reasons for wearing glasses are nearsightedness and farsightedness. Do some research to find out why people become nearsighted or farsighted.

Create the ultimate high-fashion designer glasses. Draw a picture of them and tell how much they would sell for, why they would be a good sales item, and who would be most likely to buy them.

THE GARDEN OF ABDUL GASAZI

by Chris Van Allsburg

Summary

The dog Alan runs into Abdul Gasazi's garden where it is clearly posted "No Dogs Allowed." The dog-hating magician has unsavory plans for dogs who disobey.

Vocabulary

1. invitation	6. positively	11. convinced
2. parlor	7. magician	12. detest
3. exhausted	8. tremendous	13. approached
4. distance	9. bolted	14. gust
5. absolutely	10. ignored	15. incredible

Setting Reading Purpose

Alan must "dog-sit" for a bad-mannered dog Fritz. What happens to Fritz when he enters the garden of the ill-tempered magician Abdul Gasazi?

Questions During Reading

1. (literal) Why did Miss Hester ask Alan to dog-sit? (She was going to visit her cousin Eunice, and Fritz was not invited.)
2. (inferential) Why did Alan hide his hat under his shirt while he napped? (Fritz would chew it up if he found it.)
3. (literal) What does Abdul Gasazi claim to do to dogs that he finds in his garden? (He turns them into ducks.)
4. (creative) Why do you think Gasazi does not like dogs? (Answers will vary.)

Comprehension Skill Extenders

1. Training a dog is a job that requires a lot of patience. If you had a new puppy, what things would you most want to train it to do? Why?
2. Use your best problem-solving skills to come up with a solution for the following problem:
   Your family dog Fido has an irritating habit. He chews on any shoes that he sees, even if they are on someone's feet.
   With a friend, brainstorm ways to solve the problem. List at least three possible solutions, then decide which idea is the best one and tell why.
3. If you could perform one magic trick during your lifetime, what kind of trick

would you choose? Why would you make your choice?

Curriculum Integration

Chris Van Allsburg created all his award-winning artwork for this book by using only a carbon pencil and paper. He was interested in creating balance by creating light tones and dark tones next to one another and paying careful attention to perspective.

Try your hand at creating an imaginary garden scene using only pencil and paper. Shade areas in darker when the sunlight could not be hitting. Remember to fill the page by drawing closer objects larger and objects that are farther away smaller. Consider shading all areas of the picture from the sky to the ground. Create as much necessary detail as you can.

PLAY BALL, KATE

by Sharon Gordon

Summary

A primary easy-to-read story about Kate and her baseball team.

Vocabulary

out of the park

Setting Reading Purpose

Kate plays baseball with her team at the park. What happens when Kate goes to bat?

Questions During Reading

1. (literal) Where did Kate hit the ball? (Out of the park.)
2. (inferential) How many strikes did Kate have before she hit the ball? (Two.)
3. (creative) Would you like to be on Kate's team? Why or why not? (Answers will vary.)
4. (inferential) What does Kate do when the game is over? (She takes off her hat and glove.)

Comprehension Skill Extenders

1. Read another book about a sport, and share it with a friend.
2. If you were on a baseball team, what would you like your uniform to look like? Draw and color the team cap.
3. Find and circle the baseball words in the puzzle on the reproducible student worksheet (p. 227).

Curriculum Integration

Baseball, football, and basketball are very popular sports. Take a survey of your class to find out which sport is the most popular to play and watch. Make a chart to show your results.

Baseball in Words

Name _____

Find and circle the baseball words in the wordsearch puzzle.

1. strike
2. ball
3. bat
4. hit
5. home run
6. foul
7. umpire
8. team
9. park
10. player
11. game
12. out
13. run
14. mitt

```
h  o  m  e  r  u  n  a  b  u
i  u  d  k  u  e  t  t  i  m
t  t  j  i  n  l  f  g  w  p
o  q  m  r  o  f  i  n  u  i
n  b  a  t  m  h  u  i  x  r
r  p  s  s  t  b  a  l  l  e
p  l  a  y  e  r  y  z  a  r
k  v  c  r  d  s  m  a  e  t
g  a  m  e  k  f  o  u  l  h
```

Write a sentence using four of the baseball words.

_____

_____

PLAY BALL, AMELIA BEDELIA
by Peggy Parish

Summary

When the Grizzlies need another player for their big game against the Tornadoes, Amelia Bedelia joins the team with surprising results.

Vocabulary

1. gloomy	3. attic	5. inning	7. emptied
2. measles	4. uniform	6. scorekeeper	

Setting Reading Purpose

Amelia Bedelia has a hard time understanding baseball terms. What problems does she cause the baseball team because she does not understand what they ask her to do?

Questions During Reading

1. (literal) Why couldn't Donny play baseball with the Grizzlies? (He had the measles.)
2. (inferential) What does it mean to tag the runner in baseball? (It means to touch the player with the ball to put him or her out.)
3. (literal) When the Grizzlies told Amelia Bedelia to run home, what did she do? (She went home.)
4. (inferential) Amelia Bedelia is not good at understanding many of the things people say to her. What is one thing she is good at doing? (She is good at baking.)

Comprehension Skill Extenders

1. Research to find out the home, city, or state for each of the following baseball teams:
   1. Twins
   2. Red Sox
   3. Brewers
   4. Cubs
   5. Giants
   6. Yankees
2. What do you think are the three most important skills a baseball player should have? Tell why each one is important.
3. Read *Casey at the Bat*. Write a short poem about "Amelia Bedelia at the Bat."

Curriculum Integration

Choose a favorite baseball player and record his name, league, team, position, hometown or state of team, and personal information. Share this with the rest of the class.

THE TREASURE
by Uri Shulevitz

Summary

Isaac was such a poor man that he often went to bed hungry. Three times a voice in a dream told him to search for a treasure under the bridge by the royal palace. After a long journey, a totally unexpected find creates a heartwarming climax to this age-old folktale.

Vocabulary

1. poverty
2. journey
3. wandered
4. inscription
5. contentment

Setting Reading Purpose

Isaac's strange dream keeps telling him to go to the palace to look for a treasure under the bridge. Where does he finally find his treasure?

Questions During Reading

1. (literal) How many times did Isaac dream the same dream? (Three.)
2. (inferential) Why was Isaac afraid to search for the treasure once he arrived at the bridge? (The bridge was guarded day and night.)
3. (literal) What was the dream of the captain of the guards? (To look for a treasure under Isaac's stove.)
4. (inferential) What do you think Isaac's inscription means? "Sometimes one must travel far to discover what is near." (Answers will vary.)

Comprehension Skill Extenders

1. Digging under your stove and finding an enormous amount of buried treasure would be a very unusual happening today. Pretend you are a newspaper reporter with a large city newspaper and one of the local teachers just found such a treasure. Write a news article on this unusual happening.
2. The style of the architecture in the pictures suggests that the story did not take place in the United States. Do some research to find other places where the buildings of long ago may have looked like these buildings.
3. The transportation in this story is largely by foot or horse-drawn cart. Create a list of all the methods of transportation you can find from the earliest times to the present.

Curriculum Integration

Retell this folktale in a modern-day setting. The characters and places should be similar to people and places you would come into contact with today. Illustrate the important parts of this modern-day story.

OWL MOON

by Jane Yolen

Summary

The Great Horned Owl is a beautiful, mysterious sight called up in the forest by a father and daughter owling team.

Vocabulary

1. owling
2. statues
3. faded
4. crunched
5. Great Horned Owl
6. shrugged
7. disappointed
8. stained

Setting Reading Purpose

A little girl and her dad go out very late one night to find a Great Horned Owl in the woods by their farm. What are the special rules the little girl needs to remember about owling?

Questions During Reading

1. (literal) Even though it was very late when the little girl and her dad went owling, "the sky seemed to shine." What made the sky so bright? (The moon.)
2. (inferential) When was the little girl able to talk and make noise? (After they saw the owl and were on their way home.)
3. (inferential) What is the one thing you always need to go owling? (Hope.)
4. (creative) How do you think the little girl would have felt if they had not seen an owl? (Answers will vary.)

Comprehension Skill Extenders

1. The little girl tells us in the story that when you go owling, you have to make your own heat. What are some ways people can do that?
2. In the story, we are told through the little girl that cold feels "like someone's icy hand down our back." What are five other unusual ways to finish this sentence? Cold feels like...
3. A simile is a comparison of two things using the words "like," "as," "as if." Authors use similes to paint pictures with words. Jan Yolen says of the land around the farm, "... it was as quiet as a dream." Use your imagination to complete the simile starters on the reproducible student worksheet (p. 231).

Curriculum Integration:

Put yourself in the place of the little girl. Now think of an animal you would most like to see in its natural habitat up-close. Write a short story about the experience using your animal choice in the title:

Examples:
"Elephant Moon"
"Pheasant Moon"
"Coyote Moon"

Simile Starters

Name _____

Use your imagination to complete these similes.

as LARGE as

as SOFT as

as QUICK as

as HOT AS

as DARK as

as SCARY as

AS FUNNY as

as THIN as

MUFARO'S BEAUTIFUL DAUGHTERS

by John Steptoe

Summary

Mufaro's daughters Manyara and Nyasha are both beautiful on the outside. Nyasha is also beautiful on the inside, but Manyara is greedy and spiteful. In the end, the true character of each daughter is rewarded.

Vocabulary

1. responded	8. grove	15. destination
2. ignored	9. foretold	16. transfixed
3. millet	10. acknowledges	17. descended
4. bountiful	11. garments	18. piercing
5. messenger	12. interrupted	19. chamber
6. proclaimed	13. commotion	20. enclosure
7. silhouetted	14. approaching	21. hysterically

Setting Reading Purpose

1. Mufaro has two beautiful daughters, Manyara and Nyasha. How are the two daughters different from each other?
2. Which of the two daughters do you like better? Why?

Questions During Reading

1. (literal) Manyara thinks she will be a queen some day. What does she want her sister to be? (A servant in the queen's house.)
2. (inferential) How does Manyara feel about kindness? (She thinks it is a weakness.)
3. (literal) Why did Manyara not want Nyasha to go to the king when they arrived at the great city? (She was frightened because the five-headed snake knew all her faults.)
4. (inferential) After Nyasha became queen, what was Manyara's job? (She became a servant in the queen's house.)

Comprehension Skill Extenders

1. Alphabetize the vocabulary words given for this story.
2. The animals found in Africa are different from the animals usually found in the United States. Make a list of ten animals found in Africa. Illustrate your favorite and give two facts about it.

3. Life in an African village is much different from life in the great cities. How is living in a large American city different from living on an American farm? How is it the same? Which would you prefer if you had a choice? Why?

Curriculum Integration

We can gather information about the way people lived hundreds of years ago by examining things that have been left behind. Five hundred years from now our civilization will have changed greatly. Pretend you are a scientist in the year AD 3500. What will you be able to tell about the way we live today from the things we have left behind? How do you think civilization will have changed in 500 years?

WHERE THE WILD THINGS ARE

by Maurice Sendak

Summary

Max, his imagination running wild, was sent to his room without supper. While he is there, Max travels to the land of the wild things but returns in time for supper.

Vocabulary

1. mischief
2. tumbled
3. private
4. gnashed
5. rumpus

Setting Reading Purpose

Max is sent to his room for behaving like a "wild thing." What happens when his imagination runs wild while he is in his room?

Questions During Reading

1. (literal) How was Max dressed on the night when he caused mischief? (He wore his wolf suit.)
2. (inferential) Why did Max give up being king of the Wild Things? (He was lonely for someone who loved him.)
3. (literal) What was waiting for Max when he returned from the land of the wild things?
(His supper.)
4. (inferential) What was the name of Max's private boat? (Max.)

Comprehension Skill Extenders

1. "The Wild Things" were all part of Max's imagination. Use your imagination to create your own "wild thing." Create a detailed pencil sketch, then use paint to provide bright colors on a large sheet of drawing paper.
2. Create a new ending for the story in which Max does not become lonely and return home.
3. Max created an unusual tropical room in his imagination. If your room could be changed exactly as you would like it to look, what would it look like? Describe it in detail, and draw a picture of it.

Curriculum Integration

Make a brown paper bag mask of your own personal "wild thing." Use construction paper in bright colors to create all the details. Leave holes for your eyes so you can wear the mask.

You can cut circles and fold to create three-dimensional cones for a nose, horns, etc.

You can also fold and glue strings to create parts that stick out. Use your imagination to cover the entire bag.

SAM, BANGS AND MOONSHINE
by Evaline Ness

Summary
Sam, the fisherman's daughter, had a pronounced bad habit—lying. Her consistent liberties with the truth nearly cost the lives of her beloved cat Bangs and her friend Thomas.

Vocabulary

1. reckless	7. scoured	13. sodden	19. interrupted
2. cargoes	8. diminishing	14. incredible	20. laryngitis
3. mermaid	9. desire	15. elegant	21. immense
4. chariot	10. unaware	16. African	22. wheezed
5. jungle-gym	11. torrent	17. harbor	
6. windmill	12. menacing	18. gerbil	

Setting Reading Purpose
Samantha, called Sam for short, has an unusual imagination. She makes up so many stories that people cannot believe her when she tells them things. What is the one really unbelievable bit of information she has about her cat Bangs that probably nobody would ever believe?

Questions During Reading
1. (literal) What was the name of Sam's cat? (Bangs.)
2. (inferential) What is "moonshine"? (Make-believe.)
3. (literal) Who is the one person who always believes Sam? (Thomas.)
4. (creative) Why does Sam's dad call her stories moonshine instead of lies? (Answers will vary.)

Comprehension Skill Extenders
1. Compare Sam to the boy who cried, "wolf." How are they alike and different?
2. In the story, Sam does not notice the "thick muddy clouds" that forewarn us of a storm. Brainstorm with a friend, and list as many sights, sounds, and smells as you can think of that signal a change in the weather.
3. Do research to find out the purpose of a lighthouse. Sketch what you believe the inside of one looks like.

Curriculum Integration
If you had a favorite pet gerbil and had to go on a month-long summer vacation with your family, what instructions would you leave your friend who was going to care for your pet? Be as accurate as you can. What equipment and supplies would you leave for your friend?

BIBLIOGRAPHY

Abiyoyo, Pete Seeger, Macmillan Publishing, 1986 (p. 77).

Alexander, Who Used to be Rich Last Sunday, Judith Viorst, Atheneum, 1978 (p. 185).

Amelia Bedelia, Peggy Parish, Harper Row Publishers, 1963 (p. 186).

An Evening At Alfie's, Shirley Houghes, Lothrop, Lee and Shepard Books, New York, 1984 (p. 112).

Angelina's Christmas, Katherine Holabird, Clarkson N. Potter, New York, 1985 (p. 102).

April Fool, Mary Blount Christian, Macmillan Publishing, New York, 1981 (p. 206).

Arthur's Tooth, Marc Brown, Atlantic Monthly Press, 1985 (p. 134).

Arthur's Christmas, Marc Brown, Little Brown and Co., Boston, 1984 (p. 100).

Aunt Eater Loves a Mystery, Doug Cushman, Harper and Row, New York, 1987 (p. 60).

Bad Dog, Ned Delaney, William Morrow and Co., New York, 1987 (p. 113).

Bear Shadow, Frank Asch, Prentice-Hall, 1985 (p. 138).

Big Anthony and The Magic Ring, Tomie de Paola, Harcourt, Brace, Jovanovich, 1979 (p. 82.)

The Big Sneeze, Ruth Brown, Lothrop, Lee and Shepard Books, New York, 1985 (p. 116).

The Braggin' Dragon, Bill Martin, Jr. and John Archambault, DLM Teaching Resources, Texas, 1989 (p. 32).

Caleb and Kate, William Steig, Farrar, Straus, Giroux, New York, 1977 (p. 198).

The Case of the Cat's Meow, Crosby Bonsall, Harper and Row, New York, 1965 (p. 40).

The Cat on the Dovrefell, translated by Sir George Webbe Dasent, G.P. Putnam's Sons, New York, 1979 (p. 172).

Cherries and Cherry Pits, Vera B. Williams, Greenwillow Books, 1986 (p. 106).

The Christmas Day Kitten, James Herriot, St. Martin's Press, New York, 1976, 1986 (p. 86).

The Christmas Cat, Efner T. Holmes, Harper and Row, 1976 (p.104).

Daniel O'Rourke, An Irish Tale, Gerald McDermott, Penguin Books, 1986 (p. 158).

The Day Jimmy's Boa Ate the Wash, Trinka Hakes Noble, E.P. Dutton, New York, 1980 (p. 125).

Digging Up Dinosaurs, Aliki, Crowell, 1981 (p. 16).

Dinosaurs are Different, Aliki, Thomas Y. Crowell, 1985 (p. 15).

Do Not Open, Brinton Turkle, E.P. Dutton, New York, 1981 (p. 50).

The Dream Eater, Christian Garrison, Aladdin Books, New York, 1986 (p. 174).

Drummer Hoff, adapted by Barbara Emberley, Simon and Schuster, Inc., New York, 1967 (p. 160).

Duncan and Dolores, Barbara Samuels, Bradbury Press, 1986 (p. 140).

The Fire Cat, Ester Averill, 1960 (p. 136).

A Fish in His Pocket, Denys Cazet, Orchard Books, 1987 (p. 131).

Footprints in the Refrigerator, Selma and Pauline Boyd, Franklin Watts Publishing, New York, 1982 (p. 46).

The Frankenbagel Monster, Daniel Pinkwater, E.P. Dutton, 1986 (p. 70).

The Garden of Abdul Gasazi, Chris Van Allsburg, Houghton-Mifflin, Boston, 1979 (p. 224).

The Giant Jam Sandwich, John Vernon Lord, Houghton-Mifflin, 1972 (p. 94).

The Giant's Toe, Brock Cole, Farrar, Straus, and Giroux, 1986 (p. 66).

Gorky Rises, William Steig, Farrar, Straus, and Giroux Publishing, 1980 (p. 52).

The Greedy Old Fat Man, Paul Galdone, Clarion Books, New York, 1983 (p. 182).

Gregory the Terrible Eater, Mitchell Sharmat, Macmillan, 1980 (p. 105).

Grumley the Grouch, Marjorie Weinman Sharmat, Holiday House, 1980 (p. 144).

Harald and the Giant Knight, Donald Carrick, Clarion Books, 1982 (p. 78).

Harriet's Recital, Nancy Carlson, Carolrhoda Books, Minneapolis, Minnesota, 1982 (p. 120).

Henry and the Dragon, Eileen Christelow, Clairon Press, 1984 (p. 18).

Her Majesty, Aunt Essie, Amy Schwartz, Bradbury Press, New York, 1984 (p. 188).

The Homework Caper, Joan M. Lexau, Harper and Row, New York, 1966 (p. 37).

Hooray for Snail, John Stadler, Thomas Y. Crowell Publishing, New York, 1984 (p. 216).

How Droofus the Dragon Lost His Head, Bill Peet, Houghton-Mifflin, 1971 (p. 19).

I Have A Friend, Keiko Narahashi, Macmillan Publishing, 1987 (p. 190).

I'll Fix Anthony, Judith Viorst, Harper and Row, New York, 1969 (p. 114).

It Wasn't My Fault, Helen Lester, Houghton-Mifflin Co., Boston, 1985 (p. 121).

Jam, Margaret Mahy, Atlantic Monthly Press, Boston, 1985 (p. 98).

Jesse Bear, What Will You Wear? Nancy White Carlstrom, Macmillan, 1986 (p. 148).

King of the Cats, Paul Galdone, Clarion Books, New York, 1980 (p. 157).

King Grisly-Beard, The Brothers Grimm, translated by Edgar Taylor, Farrar, Straus and Giroux, 1973 (p. 162).

Liang and the Magic Paintbrush, Demi, Holt, Rinehart and Winston, New York, 1980 (p. 58).

A Little Touch of Monster, Emily Lampert, Atlantic Monthly Press, 1986 (p. 80).

Love From Aunt Betty, Nancy Winslow Parker, Dodd, Mead, and Co., New York, 1983 (p. 96).

Love You Forever, Robert Munsch, Firefly Books, Ontario, Canada, 1986 (p. 196).

The Magician and the Dragon, David McKee, Peter Bedrick Books, 1986 (p. 26).

Making the Team, Nancy Carlson, Carolrhoda Books, Minneapolis, Minnesota, 1985 (p. 218).

Max, the Bad-talking Parrot, Patricia Brennan, Demoth, Dodd, Mead and Co., 1986 (p. 150).

Max, Rachel Isadora, Macmillan Publishing, New York, 1976 (p. 220).

Maybe a Monster, Martha Alexander, E.P. Dutton, 1968 (p. 74).

McBroom Tells a Lie, Sid Fleishman, Little, Brown, and Co., Boston, 1976 (p. 166).

McGoogan Moves the Mighty Rock, Dick Gackenbach, Harper and Row, 1981 (p. 168).

Merry Christmas, Strega Nona, Tomie de Paola, Harcourt, Brace, Jovanovich, 1986 (p. 92).

Miss Nelson Has a Field Day, Henry Allard and James Marshall, Houghton-Mifflin, Boston, 1985 (p. 214).

Morris's Disappearing Bag, Rosemary Wells, E. P. Dutton, 1988 (p. 90).

Mr. Wink and His Shadow, Ned, Dick Gackenbach, Harper and Row, 1983 (p. 210).

Mrs. Pig's Bulk Buy, Mary Rayner, Atheneum, 1981 (p. 95).

Mufaro's Beautiful Daughters, John Steptoe, William Morrow and Co., New York, 1987 (p. 232).

My Visit to the Dinosaurs, Aliki, Harper and Row, New York, 1985 (p. 23).

My Mother Never Listens to Me, Marjorie Weinman Sharmat, Albert Whitman and Co., Illinois, 1984 (p. 200).

My Dog and the Knock Knock Mystery, David Adler, Holiday House, New York, 1985 (p. 44).

My Mama Says There Aren't Any Zombies, Ghosts, Vampires, Creatures, Demons, Monsters, Fiends, Goblins or Things, Judith Viorst, Atheneum, 1973 (p. 76).

The Mysterious Giant of Barletta, Tomie de Paola, Harcourt, Brace, Jovanovich, 1984 (p. 69).

The Mystery of the Missing Red Mitten, Steven Kellogg, Dial Books, 1974 (p. 38).

Nate the Great and the Phony Clue, Marjorie Weinman Sharmat, Coward-McCann Inc., New York, 1977 (p. 49).

Nate the Great and the Sticky Case, Marjorie Weinman Sharmat, Coward, McCann and Georghegan, 1978 (p. 21).

No Friends, James Stevenson, Greenwillow Books, 1986 (p. 192).

No More Monsters For Me, Peggy Parish, Harper and Row Publishers, 1981 (p. 73).

No Ducks in Our Bathtub, Martha Alexander, Dial Books, New York, 1973 (p. 124).

Nothing Sticks Like a Shadow, Ann Tompert, Houghton-Mifflin, 1984 (p. 142).

Now One Foot, Now The Other, Tomie de Paola, The Trumpet Club, 1981 (p. 194).

Owl Moon, Jane Yolen, Philomel Books, New York, 1985 (p. 230).

Patrick's Dinosaurs, Carol Carrick, Clarion Books, 1983 (p. 25).

Penrod's Pants, Mary Blount Christian, Macmillan, 1986 (p. 149).

The Perfect Family, Nancy Carlson, Carolrhoda Books, Minneapolis, Minnesota, 1985 (p. 204).

Play Ball, Amelia Bedelia, Peggy Parish, Harper and Row, New York, 1972 (p. 228).

Play Ball, Kate, Sharon Gordon, Troll Publishing, New Jersey, 1981 (p. 226).

The Polar Express, Chris Van Allsburg, Houghton-Mifflin, 1985 (p. 85).

A Porcupine Named Fluffy, Helen Lester, Houghton-Mifflin Co., Boston, 1986 (p. 109).

Rabbit Goes to Night School, Judy Delton, Albert Whitman and Co., 1986 (p. 146).

Sam, Bangs and Moonshine, Evaline Ness, Henry Holt and Co., New York, 1966 (p. 236).

Santa's Crash-Bang Christmas, Steven Kroll, Holiday House, New York, 1977 (p. 88).

Sarah and the Dragon, Bruce Coville, J.B. Lippincott, 1984 (p. 24).

The Selfish Giant, Oscar Wilde, Picture Book Studio, Natick, Massachusetts, 1984 (p. 68).

Sidney Rella and the Glass Sneaker, Bernice Myers, Macmillan Publishing Co., New York, 1985 (p. 170).

Simon's Book, Henrick Drescher, Scholastic, Inc., New York, 1983 (p. 42).

Soup For Supper, Phyllis Root, Harper and Row, 1986 (p. 72).

Strega Nona's Magic Lessons, Tomie de Paola, Harcourt, Brace, Jovanovich, 1982 (p. 48).

Super Bowl, Leonard Kessler, Greenwillow Books, New York, 1980 (p. 213).

The Tale of Thomas Mead, Pat Hutchins, Mulberry Books, New York, 1980 (p. 164).

The Teacher From the Black Lagoon, Mike Thaler, Scholastic, New York, 1989 (p. 110).

Tell Me A Mitzi, Lore Segal, Scholastic Books, New York, 1970 (p. 202).

The Terrible Thing That Happened At Our House, Marge Blaine, Four Winds Press, 1975 (p. 208).

There's a Monster Under My Bed, James Howe, Atheneum, 1986 (p. 63).

There's No Such Thing As A Dragon, Jack Kent, Golden Press, 1975 (p. 28).

The Treasure, Uri Shelevitz, Farrar, Straus and Giroux, New York, 1978 (p. 229).

The Trouble With Dad, Babette Cole, G.P. Putnam's Sons, New York, 1985 (p. 128).

Two Strikes Four Eyes, Ned Delaney, Houghton-Mifflin Co., Boston, 1976 (p. 222).

Two Bad Ants, Chris Van Allsburg, Houghton-Mifflin, 1988 (p. 152).

Two-ton Secret, Mary Blount Christian, Albert Whitman and Company, Chicago, Illinois, 1981 (p. 54).

Tyler Toad and the Thunder, Robert L. Crowe, E.P. Dutton, 1980 (p. 154).

The Tyrannosaurus Game, Steven Kroll, Holiday House, 1976 (p. 34).

The Very Worst Monster, Pat Hutchins, Greenwillow Press, 1985 (p. 64).

Wanda and the Bumbly Wizard, James Flora, Atheneum, 1980 (p. 56).

We're Back! Hudson Talbott, Crown Publishers, Inc., New York, 1987 (p. 30).

A Weekend With Wendel, Kevin Henkes, Puffin Books, 1986 (p. 132).

Whatever Happened to the Dinosaurs? Bernard Most, Harcourt, Brace, and Jovanovich, 1984 (p. 31).

When Mother Got the Flu, Beverly Keller, Coward-McCann, Inc., New York, 1984 (p. 122).

Where the Wild Things Are, Maurice Sendak, Harper Row Publishers, Inc., 1983. (p. 234).

Why the Chicken Crossed the Road, David Macaulay, Houghton-Mifflin, Boston, 1987 (p. 126).

The Winter Wren, Brock Cole, Farrar, Strauss and Giroux, New York, 1984 (p. 178).

The Wolf's Chicken Stew, Keiko Kasza, G.P. Putnam's Sons, New York, 1987 (p. 118).

Zeralda's Ogre, Tomi Ungerer, Harper and Row, New York, 1967 (p. 180).